Replacement

W9-BWQ-422

A DIALECTIC
OF MORALS

A
DIALECTIC
OF MORALS

Towards the Foundations of
Political Philosophy

MORTIMER J. ADLER

Director, Institute for Philosophical Research,
San Francisco

FREDERICK UNGAR PUBLISHING CO.
NEW YORK

*To the students
who have helped me learn
during my years
of teaching*

TABLE OF CONTENTS

Chapter V. Psychological Presuppositions: Limitations of the Dialectic

Chapter VI. Real vs. Apparent Goods: The Reality of of Virtue

The ordering of ethics to politics and of politics to ethics, 108; the political common good as an end which is also a means to happiness, 108; an adequate understanding of happiness and virtue necessary to establish political philosophy, to defend it against *realpolitik*, and safeguard it from errors, such as "totalitarianism," 109; the nature of the state, 109; its naturalness in the order of final causality as an object of natural desire, 110; the mode of being of the state, 111; the state exists as an accident in so far as it exists in and through the habitual justice of its members, 112; the goodness of the common good, 113; the common good as identical with the state's well-being, 113; as such, the common good is the end of government, government being its productive means analogous to the relation of virtue and happiness, 114; the common good as a whole of goods, 114; the major principles of political theory, 115; the moral classification of governmental forms as unequally good, Democracy being best, 116; the challenge of *realpolitik* and of "totalitarianism" can be met only by the dialectical cure for moral skepticism, 116.

CHAPTER I.

INTRODUCTION: THE DIALECTICAL TASK.

IN ST. THOMAS AND THE GENTILES I tried to define the
obligations of perennial philosophy in the twentieth century. Philosophy may be perennial, but its work changes according to the cultural
conditions in which the philosopher lives and thinks. In its Greek
beginnings, philosophy arose out of the dialectical efforts of Plato and
Aristotle to clarify and order the welter of opinion. They struggled
not only with the sophists to divide the line between knowledge and
opinion; but they also moved in the realm of opinion to distinguish
the true from the false; and, in their patient consideration of pre-Socratic thought, they both tried, though differently, to convert right opinion into knowledge by making it evident to reason. Although the result
of their work was the establishment of philosophy as a body of knowledge, founded on principles and developed by demonstrations, we
must not forget that, in their day, the mode of their work was primarily
dialectical. In saying this I do not overlook the demonstrative or
scientific achievements of Plato and Aristotle; but those must be regarded as secondary, for the first work of pioneers is to stake out the
land, to clear away the brush, to prepare the soil, and to dig for firm
foundations. Only thereafter can a city be planned, buildings raised,
and interiors decorated. The Platonic dialogues certainly reveal an
intellectual pioneer at work; but no less do the so-called "scientific"
works of Aristotle, for they are primarily records of exploration and
discovery. Rather than orderly expositions of accomplished knowledge,
they are, not only in their opening chapters but throughout, dialectical
engagements with adversaries, wrestlings with the half-truths of error
and opinion in order to set the whole truth forth.

1

Under the altered cultural circumstances of the Middle Ages, philosophy lived a different sort of life. With few exceptions, the mediaeval philosophers dwelt in the domain Plato and Aristotle had won from the wilderness. The fields having been cleared and the foundations completed, the philosopher now had a different sort of work to do. Accepting the ground-plan, he proceeded to erect the mansions of philosophy, each well ordered to the others, and in each an orderly disposition of many rooms. The architectural achievement of the mediaeval philosophers extended even to exterior facades and to the detail of furnishings within. And in all this work, the primary mode of procedure was demonstrative rather than dialectical. In contrast to the writings of Plato and Aristotle, the philosophical literature of the Middle Ages is expository rather than exploratory. It proceeds by steps of analysis and synthesis. The so-called "deductive" character of mediaeval thought must not be taken to mean that mediaeval philosophers regarded philosophy as primarily or exclusively deductive, but rather as signifying that they were no longer in the pioneering stage. The inductive work, which is necessarily first, had already been well done by the Greeks. Again I must point out that, in emphasizing the demonstrative mode of mediaeval thought, I am not overlooking its dialectical phases. But the dialectical efforts of the Middle Ages were mainly in new territory, in theology rather than philosophy, and, of course, in the borderlands between philosophy and theology. And even where, within the sphere of purely philosophical questions, there is the obviously dialectical procedure of objection and reply, the dialectic is defensive rather than exploratory. It is not undertaken as a way of discovering the truth, but rather as a way to purify the truth of admixed errors, or to assimilate to knowledge the truth that is contained in errors. In every aspect and at every stage of this undertaking, the philosopher regards himself as having a wealth of well-established knowledge—an inheritance he must husband against loss or decay, a fortune he must defend against the foes of truth, an endowment not only to live on and by, but to increase by using it well.

Now the modern followers of Aristotle and St. Thomas,—or, for that matter, the followers of Plato and St. Bonaventure,—should not neglect the fact that the cultural situation in which they find themselves is neither Greek nor mediaeval. The most dismal failure of all modern "scholasticism" is its failure to be modern. This is true not only of the second-hand text-books which try to be even more demonstrative and less dialectical than the great mediaeval works, whose intellectual achievement they reflect dimly, whose living rigor becomes in the copy a *rigor mortis*. With some exceptions, it is true even of the work of the best Thomists, from John of St. Thomas to the present day.[1]

The reason for this is the failure to see precisely the way in which modern culture imposes upon the philosopher a situation analogous to, not the same as, the one in which Plato and Aristotle did their work. It is not merely that the cultural aggrandizement of the investigative or phenomenological sciences has gradually threatened the very existence of philosophy and has progressively worked to dispossess it of its ancient home; worse, and in consequence, the prevalence of positivism today requires the philosopher to face an audience radically skeptical of anything he may say, doubtful even that he can say anything worth listening to at all. I am assuming, of course, that a philosopher who is alive today should try to talk to his contemporaries, and by this I mean an audience much wider than the inner circle of his like-minded fellows in the philosophical enterprise. This is not the living philosopher's only obligation, but if he is concerned with the life of philosophy in modern culture, it is his primary one. To discharge it, he must proceed dialectically, not demonstratively, and his dialectical efforts must resemble the Greek rather than the mediaeval mode of argument. Though he regret the fact that history's progressive spiral seems to throw him back to an earlier stage, he must return to the pioneer work of the Greeks. He must once again

---

1. If we consider carefully the character of these exceptions—their philosophic mood and temper—they illustrate, by contrast to the rest of "scholasticism," what it means for philosophers to remember the thirteenth without forgetting the twentieth century. Confining myself to the field of moral philosophy, I should cite as striking exceptions—striking in themselves and also striking because it is only in the very recent past that such work has occurred—the writings of Jacques Maritain (such as *True Humanism* and *Scholasticism and Politics*) and of Yves Simon (especially noteworthy in this connection is his *Nature and Functions of Authority*); and I must also mention the work of Father Walter Farrell.

try to be primitively inductive about the basic philosophical truths.[1a]

I describe the motion of history as the path of a spiral, because the same ground is never retraced. Unlike the simpler cyclical motion which returns to the same place, progress along a spiral reaches an analogous place—both the same and different. This is illustrated by the fact that the contemporary follower of Aristotle and St. Thomas cannot do *exclusively* either the sort of work which Aristotle did, or the sort done by St. Thomas. He must do both sorts, and in that very fact he at once resembles and differs from each of them. Like

---

1a. In *St. Thomas and the Gentiles* (Milwaukee, 1938), I wrote: "Far from making every effort to join issue with those who differ from us, we have, in my judgment, not even begun to make an effort properly directed and properly proportionate to the task at hand. We have been loath to absent ourselves from the felicity of moving further into the interior of philosophical thought, when there is pressing work to be done on the border, the arduous and lowly work of the pioneer. The borderland I speak of is marked by the issue between those who hold, as we do, that philosophy is a field of knowledge in which there can be perennial truth and those who deny it" (p. 20). In this earlier work I tried to find a parallel for our task in the sort of dialectical work St. Thomas did against the gentiles in the sphere of faith. I now think a better parallel is to be found in the dialectic of Plato and Aristotle against the sophists, because the ancient effort was, and the modern effort must be, entirely within the sphere of reason.

In saying that the modern effort must be entirely within the sphere of reason, I am thinking of what I regard as the primary task of philosophy in the contemporary world—to win respect for itself in a culture that is predominantly positivist. I hope it will be understood that this is not incompatible with the general notion of a characteristically Christian philosophy—the work of reason elevated by faith—for although faith seems to have been indispensable for the mediaeval discovery of truths not known to the ancient pagans, the truths, once discovered, are possessed by reason and can, therefore, be made acceptable to the reason of modern pagans. For the most part, *Christian* philosophy, because its truths are rational, can be taught to pagans even though it could not have been initially developed by them. There is, however, one profound limitation on the foregoing statement, which is crucially relevant to the present undertaking, namely, the fact that Christian moral philosophy is not, and cannot be, purely a possession of reason, because as *practical* wisdom it is necessarily guided by faith and subalternated to moral theology. (M. Maritain has completely analyzed this point in *Science and Wisdom*, New York, 1940: Part II.) The doctrines of man's fall, redemption, and salvation, are theological, not philosophical. Since in the practical order we are concerned with ends and means, we cannot neglect the difference between the end as declared by faith and as known by natural reason; nor can we ignore the fact that natural means are insufficient for a supernatural end; they may not even be sufficient for a natural end, if the "natural man" is a hypothetical creature who does not exist. But even though a purely natural moral philosophy is not the whole truth, taken *theoretically*, and even though a purely rational morality may be *practically* false because of its theoretic inadequacy, we must nevertheless begin our dialectical undertaking with what reason *alone* can accomplish. If we succeed in winning the moral skeptic to the path of reason, and if we take him with us as far as reason can go, it will *then* be time enough to ask where we are; for *then*, as *not now*, he may be willing and prepared to consider the relation of theology to philosophy, of faith to reason, in the practical order. The reader should, therefore, understand why our present objective is the induction of Greek, and not *distinctively* Christian, moral principles.

St. Thomas, the contemporary Aristotelian must continue the constructive work that the Middle Ages began so well and did so much of—the systematic and demonstrative elaboration of philosophical knowledge.[2] Like Aristotle, the contemporary Thomist, because he is living in the modern world, must undertake the primary dialectical task of making evident the most rudimentary philosophical truths.[3] And because we are obligated today to do both sorts of work, we can do neither well unless as we do the one, we are always mindful of the other. When perennial philosophy shakes off the dead skin of scholasticism, and really comes to live in a modern metamorphosis, the event will be signified by a renewal of the dialectical enterprise with which philosophy originated in the Greek period, as well as by the renovation of the edifice which the Middle Ages raised upon Greek foundations. And each—the renewal and the renovation—will penetrate the other.

In this essay I am going to try to exemplify—even though inadequately and remotely—what I mean by the modern analogue of Greek philosophical work. I am going to try to proceed dialectically against those who say there is no moral knowledge; who say that

----

2. I am not forgetting that this process cannot occur, *today*, in exactly the same mood or manner as in the Middle Ages. Since the aim is certainly not just to repeat the mediaeval construction, we must attempt further and more detailed analyses, and these must take account of every genuine advance in knowledge, and every sound critical insight, which the modern world has gained. We may even find it necessary to tear down some parts of the mediaeval building and to reconstruct it, in order to let modern light in, to ventilate it properly, and to make it truly habitable by a modern mind. And in emphasizing here the demonstrative and expository character of such constructive, or reconstructive, work, I do not mean to exclude dialectical procedures entirely, for they are necessarily involved. But the kind of dialectic by which a living Thomism continues to grow is mediaeval rather than Greek in type—that is, it is not primary and inductive, but secondary and auxiliary to the deeper penetration of truths already known.

3. Here, too, there is a difference in the mood and manner in which a similar task is undertaken; for whereas Aristotle was genuinely exploring the philosophical field by dialectical methods, and discovering truths by inductive procedures, we are not learning these elementary truths for the first time, but rather are trying to teach them to a world which denies their possibility. We must, therefore, use the dialectical method and the inductive procedure as instruments of instruction rather than of discovery. It is highly probable, of course, that what occurs as a discovery of truth for those whom we try to teach may be more than a mere re-discovery for us, the teachers. Since the cultural context of the modern world is different, since the steps we must take in reaching the same truths are not precisely those which Aristotle took, the truths themselves may be seen in a new light; and it is even possible that, as a result of such efforts, new truths may be discovered.

good and bad, right and wrong, are entirely matters of opinion; who say, as a consequence, that might makes right in the sphere of politics. My aim is not merely negative, though in an effort to establish first principles, my arguments will usually take the form of the *reductio ad impossibile.* The destructive force of such arguments is, however, for the sake of a positive result—the inductive perception of the most elementary truths.

There are many other topics which offer similar occasions for dialectical work and, in every case, there is a parallelism between the contemporary situation and that of 5th century Greece. Thus, where the ancient sophists denied knowledge and said that everything was a matter of opinion, the modern positivists deny that there is any knowledge beyond or outside of the so-called positive sciences, or, in other words, they say that philosophy is opinion; as, in the ancient world, there were those who said that the truth was merely what appeared to be the case, and hence relative to each individual, so today there are similar relativists about truth; as then there were those who denied any way of knowing except by the senses, so now the intellect is denied as a distinct faculty of knowing; as among the pre-Socratic physicists there were those who regarded the sensible world as exclusively an affair of flux and becoming, in which there were no enduring entities, such as substances, so those who regard themselves as philosophical interpreters of modern physics also deny substances, and view the sensible world as nothing but a process of events. In each of these cases, the dialectical task confronting us is analogous to the task which Plato and Aristotle faced: to establish, *inductively,* the distinction between knowledge and opinion and to show that philosophy is knowledge; to establish that truth is objective and the same for all men because it is an agreement of the mind with reality; to establish the distinction between sensitive and intellectual knowing, and to show that man knows things that he cannot know by his senses alone; to establish the existence of substances as the subjects of change.

I have chosen the topic of moral knowledge,—the objectivity and universality of moral standards,—because it is so relevant to this critical moment in our culture. It will not be necessary to engage in distinct dialectical enterprises for the separate fields of ethics and politics. If skepticism about moral truths can be overcome at all, if any judgments about good and bad can be shown to have the status of knowledge, then a foothold is won for political as well as for ethical standards. How much of the traditional content of ethics and politics can be drawn from the few principles we are able to establish dialectically, is something which remains to be seen.

Let me describe the state of mind which I call moral skepticism. It is not a total skepticism. There is no question about the validity of the natural and social sciences. These sciences describe phenomena; their generalizations can always be verified by reference to particular sense experiences; and even though the truths they achieve are not "final" or "absolute,"—but always relative to the data now at hand, —these truths are, nevertheless, objective in the sense that they are matters upon which all competent judges can be expected to agree in the light of the evidence. In contrast to the affirmation of the natural and social sciences is the denial of the moral sciences—the branches of practical philosophy traditionally known as ethics and politics. This denial is made on any one of three counts: (1) it may be involved in the general denial of philosophical knowledge, for this would eliminate the possibility of practical philosophy as a body of knowledge;[4] (2) even though some branches of philosophy are admitted as a kind of knowledge, such as logic and mathematics,[5] there is no philosophical knowledge which reports the nature of things; and to the extent that ethics and politics depend upon theoretic philosophy, they are involved in this denial; (3) whether or not theoretic philosophy has the status of knowledge, there cannot be any practical philosophy, for that would be "normative" or "evaluative" and such judgments can never be more than opinion.

The position of the moral skeptic can, therefore, be summarized

---

4. It should be noted that what is being denied is not politics as one of the social sciences, but politics as a branch of practical, or moral, philosophy.

5. They are regarded as regulative disciplines, as formal sciences, whereas the natural and social sciences are regarded as sciences of the real, even though the only reality be phenomenal.

as follows. He says that about moral matters (good and bad, right and wrong, in the action of individuals or groups) there is only opinion, not knowledge. Or he says that moral judgments are entirely subjective, i. e., having truth or meaning only for the individual who makes them. Or he says that moral judgments are relative to the customs of a given community, at a given time and place, in which case, although the judgments made by an individual may be measured in terms of their conformity to the *mores* of the group, the *mores* themselves have no truth or meaning except for the group which has instituted them. Or he says that all norms or standards are entirely conventional, whether instituted by the will of the community or by the will of individuals; and this amounts to saying that moral judgments are ultimately willful prejudices, expressions of emotional bias, of temperamental predilection. That these several statements all come to the same thing can be seen in the fact that in every case the same thing is being denied, namely, the possibility of making moral judgments which are true for all men everywhere, unaffected not only by their individual differences but also by the diversity of the cultures under which they live.[6]

The issue is quite clear. The dialectical task is set. It will not do for the philosopher simply to reiterate his claims concerning the universality of moral truths, the self-evidence or demonstrability of the principles and conclusions of ethics and politics. Nor is it sufficient for him to be passive in their defense, however willing he may be to answer objections; for the moral skeptic, especially if he is a positivist, is not entirely wrong in charging that every answer begs the ultimate question—the question whether anything the philosopher says is more than opinion. In this situation, the philosopher must be aggressive. He must engage the moral skeptic on his own grounds. He must open his adversary's mind to a perception of the truth,— if not to the whole truth, at least to certain aspects of the truth which will function as seed to be cultivated. This is what I mean by an inductive use of dialectic.

---

6. Two other denials are implicit here: (1) the denial of a natural moral law, in consequence of which morality becomes entirely conventional; and (2) the denial that moral judgments are expressions of reason, rather than of will or passion.

I have elsewhere discussed the prevalence and causes of moral skepticism among the educated classes in America today.[7] It is the position of most of the teachers in our secular colleges and universities, and naturally enough it becomes the position of their students. I have already mentioned one of the causes, namely, positivism; but there are two others which, although consequences or aspects of positivism, should be separately noted. One is the kind of psychology that is taught: the only *knowledge* we are supposed to have concerning human nature comes to us from the laboratory or the clinic.[8] The other is the emphasis, in the teaching of all the social sciences, upon the diversity of *mores:* each culture consists of its own peculiar system of values, and there is no way of evaluating cultures themselves, no way of judging them, without begging the whole question, for such judgments would have to be made in terms of the "postulates" or assumptions underlying a given culture.[9]

Though the causes may be superficially different, in so far as they reflect peculiarly modern conditions, the ultimate sources of our moral skepticism are essentially the same as those responsible for the teaching

----

7. In "This Pre-War Generation," an article in Harper's Magazine, October, 1940 (No. 1085, pp. 524-534).

8. The neglect or denial of what, in contrast, I would call philosophical psychology results in the denial or, what is just as bad, the misconception of man's rationality and freedom. The relevance of such denials or misconceptions to moral skepticism will become apparent in the course of the dialectic.

9. This can be most strikingly exemplified by the position of those political scientists who are willing to urge us to fight for democracy, but who refuse to argue that the principles of democracy are intrinsically, and absolutely, right, or even objectively better than the principles of totalitarianism. Adopting the views of *realpolitik*, they must regard this issue as nothing more than a struggle between "ideologies"—the one to which we are devoted not being objectively better than the other, but better-for-us because it is ours by the accident of cultural location.

Let me add here that all the facts of cultural anthropology must be admitted. The moral skeptic often supposes these facts to be absolutely incompatible with the position that some moral judgments are true for all men everywhere. But this is not the case. The truths of moral philosophy, the principles of ethics and politics, do not require us to shut our eyes to any facts about human life and human society. The precise relation between the universality and absoluteness of moral truth, on the one hand, and the diversity and relativity of the *mores*, on the other hand, will become apparent, I hope, in the course of the dialectic.

of the Greek sophists.[10] The parallelism is extraordinary. In both cases, the issue is a matter of general concern because it deeply affects the education of youth; in both cases, the philosopher is opposed to the dominant elements in the teaching profession.

The dialectic of morals which I shall now proceed to outline is not an imaginary intellectual process. It is rather a distillation of actual arguments which President Hutchins and I have had with students in courses devoted to the reading of great works in ethics and politics. The situation we face year after year is the same; the students are, for the most part, moral skeptics. They challenge us to try to change their minds. In meeting that challenge we have found certain modes of argument most effective. The only invention involved in the development of this dialectic is the precise ordering of the steps. It is necessary to find those points of departure which make contact with the minds we are trying to move; and it is necessary to sustain the motion, once started, by linking the steps in a tight sequence, so that no leaps are required. Most of the steps are provided by the tradition, especially by Plato and Aristotle, but

---

10. The position of Thrasymachus in *The Republic*, and the views attributed to Protagoras and other sophists, in the writings of Plato and Aristotle, are perfect expressions of moral skepticism. Although the thing we call "positivism" is typically modern, because it arises in modern times with the gradual distinction of science from philosophy, there is a Greek analogue in so far as the sophists were not total skeptics. All but the most extreme among them, such as Cratylus, were willing to admit that we had knowledge of the physical world; in fact, they used such knowledge to make their point that in moral matters only opinions prevailed. They were fond of saying that fire burns in the same way in both Greece and Persia, both a hundred years ago and today, but the laws of Greece and Persia are not the same nor are the customs of antiquity and of the present. Of nature, because it is nature and has a persistent uniformity independent of human will, there can be knowledge, but there can be only opinions on moral matters, because they are not natural, because they are entirely conventional, entirely dependent on human institution, entirely expressions of will. The sophists knew a great deal about the variety of customs; obviously impressed by the relativity of *mores*, they made the same false supposition that is made today, namely, the incompatibility of such facts with the possibility of universal moral principles. Finally, it can even be said that the sophists' view of human nature, without benefit of experimental research or clinical investigation, emphasized, as does our current scientific psychology, the will or passions, rather than the reason, and made the sensitive faculty the primary, if not the exclusive, principle of human knowledge. The main points of this analogy between the ancient sophists and the contemporary moral skeptics is confirmed, from the other side, by the late Professor F. C. S. Schiller, the follower of William James and John Dewey who, more explicitly than they, avowed the moral skepticism which is implicit in pragmatism. Vd. his essay, *From Plato to Protagoras*, in which Schiller sides with Protagoras (in *Studies in Humanism*, New York, 1907: Ch. II).

we have found it necessary to produce an ancient play of the mind in modern dress.

The whole dialectic cannot be accomplished in a single sequence. Several motions are involved, some from opposite directions, but all converging on the point to be established. What I am going to set down in each case must be regarded as the bare plot for a dialogue between teacher and student. To write such dialogues out in full— to report in detail the actual sessions in which these arguments took place—would require more skill than I possess, and more space than is available. Furthermore, what is essentially the same intellectual process can take place in countless different ways, according to the contingent circumstances of actual discussion. These dialectical plots can never be enacted in the same way, but they are, nevertheless, common to a wide variety of conversations about such themes.

CHAPTER II.

PREFERENCE AND PLEASURE: INDUCTION
OF A PRINCIPLE.

LET US BEGIN with an indisputable fact. No one can deny the fact of *preference*. If there is anyone who says he has never preferred one thing to another, never done one thing rather than another, we must inquire, then, whether he has ever experienced desire at all, of any sort. And if he admits having had the experience of desire, he can certainly be made to understand the difference between something which would satisfy that desire and something which would not. Hence, he can at least imagine a situation in which, given a certain desire, he would *prefer* one thing to another. But it is unlikely that we shall be compelled to persuade anyone about the fact of preference—certainly not about its existence, though, perhaps, about its significance. That, then, can be our starting point.[11]

The fact of preference can be set forth in a simple formula which describes every case: X, who is a man, prefers A to B, and here A and B can either be objects or courses of action. In fact, whatever A and B stand for, whoever prefers A to B is saying that A is *better than* B. The fact of *preference* is thus seen to be equivalent to the judgment of *better-than*.

But the student will object, of course, that he does not know what "better-than" means; he has admitted the fact of preference, but he has not admitted that there is anything really good and bad, or better and worse. If "better-than" means no more than "preferred-

---

11. I should like to observe here that the fact of *preference* plays a role in the dialectic of morals like the role played by the fact of *change* in the dialectic of substance. If anyone persist in denying the existence of change, it will be impossible, I think, to induce that person to see the necessity for there being a multiplicity of individual substances. So, too, if anyone really persist in denying that men exercise preferences, it will be impossible to carry him any distance at all into the field of morals.

by-me," says the student, then the equivalence of the fact of preference with the judgment of better-than can be conceded; but not otherwise.

At this point let us focus the whole issue on the fact of preference. Let us consider two men, X and Y, both of whom, as a matter of fact, prefer A to B. Let X be a moral skeptic, such as the student is, who claims that in expressing this preference he is expressing nothing more than his private opinion; X, furthermore, denies that there are any principles behind this judgment of preference which might lead any other man, in the same situation, to judge in the same way. And, for the sake of contrast, let Y be a moralist who claims that his reasons for preferring A to B include universally valid principles which set up an order of goods, of things as better and worse, for any man at any time and place.

Now it will be observed that the two men, X and Y, agree upon the fact of preference, though they disagree in the explanation they give in answer to the question, Why do you prefer A to B? We have not yet heard the moral skeptic's explanation of his preference, but we know it must be different from the moralist's. It should be noted, moreover, that it makes no difference whether X and Y both prefer A to B, or whether they make opposite choices here, for in either case the fact of preference remains to be explained, and it is the difference in the explanations which matters. Let there be no doubt on this point, for if the explanation given by the moral skeptic is not radically and irreducibly different from the explanation given by the moralist, there is no issue.

We must, therefore, ask the student to explain preference. He may, of course, answer that there is no explanation, that he never has any grounds whatsoever for preferring one thing to another. If he says this, he must be asked why, then, does he prefer one thing to another. Should he reply that, in fact, he does not really prefer one thing to another—that, when he appears to choose A rather than B, it is only in the way in which one tosses a coin to make a decision, or in the way in which one makes a blindfold choice between the right hand and the left—it will be necessary to remind him that he is now denying what before he admitted. He was not originally asked to agree that he, in fact, *did* one thing rather than another, but that he *preferred* to do this rather than that. In short, he cannot admit the fact of preference and deny that he regards one thing as better than another, even if that means only better-for-him. Hence, he cannot refuse to give us some explanation of his preferences, some account of how or why he regards one thing as somehow better than another.

At this point the student can be helped to a decision by being presented with the following dilemma: *either* what is preferred is something which any rational being would prefer under those circumstances, something which in the nature of the case is better than the rejected alternative, *or* the preference expresses nothing more than this individual's feelings at the moment. The student will recognize at once that if he take the first horn of the dilemma, he is conceding the existence of moral knowledge, a rational judgment about what is good and bad, which has truth for any man. Since the existence of moral knowledge is to be proved, the student quite properly takes the other horn of the dilemma.

Let us now make the student's position explicit He is saying that he prefers A to B, because he *likes* A. Furthermore, he wishes to be understood as saying that his liking A is entirely a matter of his present state of feelings about A and B; tomorrow he might like B. And he would not be at all surprised to find that other men liked B when he liked A, or conversely; nor would he attempt to argue with them about this difference in their tastes, for about liking and disliking there can be no argument.

We have now discovered an interesting point, which the student should recognize. The moral skeptic, when urged to explain the fact of preference, becomes a hedonist. In order to avoid saying that he prefers A because his *reason* tells him it is really better, he says that it is entirely a matter of his *feelings*—feelings of pleasure and displeasure. Nothing new has been introduced into the discussion by the use of the words "pleasure" and "displeasure" for the student will admit that "A pleases me" or "A gives me pleasure" is the verbal equivalent of "I like A." Hence, with the student's consent, we can conclude that a moral skeptic is one who explains preference in terms of feelings of pleasure and displeasure—feelings which are entirely subjective, operating for this individual and at this moment in this situation.

If, now, we ask the student *why* he likes A, why it pleases him, he may protest the question. There is no why for liking. The feeling of pleasure is an immediate experience which determines preference, and that is all there is to it. The student may even tell us that we have no right to ask *why*, for the very question implies that there are reasons; whereas he has already told us there are none unless the feeling of pleasure itself be called a "reason" for preference. If we wish to use the word "reason" that way, then pleasure and displeasure, he reiterates, are the only reasons for preference.

But there is still some room for inquiry about these feelings of pleasure and displeasure. We admit that there is no problem if A pleases and B displeases. In this simple case, the principle of preference is clear: pleasure is preferred to displeasure. And no further explanation need be given of this principle, for we can agree with the student that it is a principle of animal conduct: animals embrace what they like, and avoid what they dislike. That can be taken as a scientific fact. And although with some of the lower animals their likes and dislikes are instinctive (and so common to all members of the species), in the case of man, instinct is either weak or non-existent, and human likes and dislikes are matters of individual conditioning. Hence, we cannot as a matter of scientific knowledge declare what all men will like or dislike. Therefore, on moral matters there is only opinion.

All cases are not, however, so simple. We must ask the student to consider a situation in which he has often found himself; he likes both A and B. Whereas in the simple case first given, B was positively displeasing, here B is pleasing. Now what is the principle of preference? The student will answer, as it seems he must, that in this case he prefers A because A is more pleasing—he likes A more than B.

We have thus arrived at a second principle of preference. The first principle was: A is considered better-than-B-for-me whenever A gives me pleasure and B displeasure. The second principle is: A is considered better-than-B-for-me whenever A gives me more, and B less, pleasure. The question now is whether a genuinely new criterion has been introduced. According to the first principle, pleasure was the only criterion of preference. The second principle appears to add a new criterion: quantity of pleasure. To be sure we understand this new criterion, let us consider another case in which the alternatives are A and C, on the one hand, and B, on the other. Let it be supposed that B is more pleasing than either A or C taken separately, but that together A and C will give more pleasure than B. Applying the standard of quantity, the student tells us that in such a situation he will prefer A and C to B.

Would any other man make the same judgment? we ask. Yes, says the student, faced by a choice between more and less pleasure,— whether the greater quantity be simply the greater intensity of one pleasure over another, or the summation of two pleasures which exceeds a single pleasure,—any man would prefer more or less. Is this, we ask, a matter of human instinct or of human reason? Why is more of what we like better than less? The student replies that he doesn't know whether it is instinct or reason, but that it makes no difference. Animals not only seek pleasure and avoid displeasure, but they also prefer more pleasure to less. This is simply the fact, and it applies to men as well as other animals. It is an ultimate fact, about which no further whys can be asked.

But, we persist, the criterion of quantity as a principle of preference raises further questions which must be faced. In the first place, the student must now admit that pleasure is not the *only* criterion of preference. Quantity is an additional criterion, and a more ultimate criterion, since one pleasure is preferred to another *because* of quantity, not one quantity to another *because* of pleasure. The student objects, saying that more pleasure is better simply because it is more *pleasure*, not because it is *more*. To argue this question, let us consider a case. One is faced with a choice between a bag containing three apples and a bag containing two. One likes apples. Both bags are obtainable with equal ease. Let us further suppose that one's appetite for apples is equal to eating three of them in succession. The preference, then, for the bag of three must be based on the difference in quantity, on the fact that more of the same is better than less. Hence whenever there is an alternative between two things which please in the same way, pleasure itself cannot determine preference, but only something which measures the pleasure, namely, quantity. And if quantity measures pleasure, and if it is on such measurement of pleasure that preference is based, then quantity is a more ultimate criterion than pleasure. But the student counters by asking us to consider an opposite case, in which pleasure appears to measure quantity. In this case, one is faced with a choice between two bags, containing an equal number of objects, let us say, three apples and three bitter pills Of course there is no problem here, we hasten to admit, because here the choice will be made in terms of pleasure as against displeasure The student then revises the situation, supposing the bags to contain three apples and three bars of chocolate, both of which give pleasure, and let us even add, he says, that the pleasure they give is of the same sort. The student will soon realize that his case has now betrayed him, for if any preference is to be expressed it will have to be in favor of the greater pleasure to be obtained from the unit of apple as against the unit of chocolate, or conversely. Given an equal sum of such units in the two bags, and given the same rate of diminishing increment of pleasure from successive units, he must, according to his own principles, prefer the bag which contains the object, any unit of which gives him *greater* pleasure. That pleasure never measures quantity, as quantity measures pleasure, is thus summarily seen in the fact that there is no ground at all for preference between equal quantities of the same pleasure, and in the fact that whenever one quantity is preferred to another it is because the one preferred gives *more* pleasure, not simply pleasure.

Granted, the student may now be willing to say, but what is the significance of all this? There are two answers: first, that pleasure and displeasure are by themselves, taken without qualification or measurement, insufficient to explain all the facts of preference; second, the criterion of quantity, as irreducible to the criterion of pleasure, and as more ultimate than pleasure because measuring it, may help us to modify the extreme character of the student's moral skepticism. To show him this, we go on to the next point.

If pleasure, as against displeasure, were the only criterion of preference, the student could persist in holding his original position that every moral judgment (every judgment of A-better-than-B-for-me) was entirely individual, made by him at this moment according to the state of his feelings, and hence subjective, hence an opinion that has no relevance to anyone else faced with the same alternatives. But if instead of A representing a source of pleasure and B a source of displeasure, we let A represent a greater, and B a lesser, pleasure, then is the judgment of preference for A over B subjective in the same way? Yes, says the student, because the fact that I find greater pleasure in A at this moment does not mean that anyone else does, or need to, or even that I will tomorrow. This we must grant, but that the principle itself is not subjective is our real contention. We are not trying to say that two different individuals, or the same individual at different times, will find greater pleasure in A. We are saying, however, that whenever anyone finds greater pleasure in one thing than in another, that is the thing he will prefer. And this principle of preference is absolutely universal. It holds for all men everywhere and at all times. One might formulate this principle as follows: if anything at all is good, a larger amount of good is better than a smaller. Even the man who says that the only good is pleasure is nevertheless compelled to agree that he would be a fool if, in pursuing such goods, he ever took less pleasure when more was available. Here, then, is a moral rule binding all men. Let us state it as a moral rule, in the imperative mood: Always choose the greater good. Agreeing for the moment that pleasure is the only good, this command can be stated declaratively: A man *should* always choose more pleasure in preference to less And this moral judgment, however stated, and with whatever meaning is assigned to the word "good," appears to be universally true, a matter of knowledge, not opinion. *Hence when A stands merely for "more pleasure" and B stands for "less pleasure," the words "for me" can be omitted from the judgment that A is better than B.*

Not so fast, says the student. Either you did not need the criterion of quantity to make this point, or I do not understand its significance. You could have made the same point, he goes on to explain, in terms of pleasure and displeasure. For if A stands for "source of pleasure" and B for "source of displeasure," then the words "for me" can also be omitted from the statement that A is better than B. Here, too, there is a universal moral rule, if you wish to call it such: Always choose pleasure rather than displeasure. And if you want to substitute the words "good" and "evil" as verbal equivalents, you can say: Always choose good rather than evil. But such statements are either tautologies, or they do no more than merely report the facts of animal behavior, namely, that all animals seek pleasure and avoid displeasure, or seek more pleasure rather than less. All that you have done, he tells us, is to disguise a scientific fact by putting it into the linguistic form of a command, or a moral injunction, using the word "should." What is the point of saying that men *should* do what they cannot fail to do? Is there any meaning to a moral rule which cannot be violated? In fact, have we the right to call anything a moral rule, a rule of conduct, unless it can somehow be violated? For otherwise the moral rule would not be a basis for judging men as good and bad, right and wrong in their actions, according as they conform to or transgress the rule. The usual conception of the moralist's position certainly involves not only universal rules, but the possibility of making such judgments about men in terms of them. Furthermore, the whole discussion is off the point, because the real judgment of preference is made by me here and now in this situation, and is determined not by such universal principles as "pleasure is always better than displeasure" or "more pleasure is always better than less pleasure," but by my present, thoroughly individual feelings about objects I like and dislike, or like more and less intensely.

By such objections, the student has brought the issue into clearer focus. He has raised two questions, not one, and these must be separated. The first has to do with the point about the violability of moral rules. In a sense he is right that an inviolable moral rule is not a statement of what *should* be done, but of what in fact is the case about the nature of human conduct. There must be some distinction, he rightly insists, between moral and natural necessity, between a moral statement and one made by the psychologist as a descriptive scientist. The second question concerns the subjectivity of any actual preference; and here again the student is right if the preference is solely determined by how he feels about A and B. Even if the judgment, *that men should always prefer a greater good,* were truly a moral rule, because violable, it would have no significance practically if, as between A and B, preference were entirely determined by how an individual felt about A and B, which he liked more, for example. Let us consider these two points in order.

The student's objections, it will be remembered, arose from his inability to see why we were so insistent about the criterion of quantity. That can now be explained to him, perhaps, in terms of the fact that it makes it easier to formulate a moral rule which shall be at once both universal and capable of violation. If we had used the criterion of pleasure, as against displeasure, to formulate a rule (e. g., that pleasure *should always* be preferred), it would have been extremely difficult, perhaps even impossible, to show that this rule was not a statement of observable fact, confirmed by all psychological investigations; for even the pathological cases of masochism are generally understood as men taking pleasure, as opposed to displeasure, in sensations of pain. Let us see, therefore, whether the criterion of quantity helps us.

We must take a more complicated case than any we have so far considered. Let A and C stand for a sum of pleasures greater than the single pleasure B. But let the conditions be such that whereas A and B are pleasures capable of immediate enjoyment, C is a pleasure that cannot be enjoyed until sometime in the future, though it can be imagined now. Furthermore, let the future enjoyment of C depend upon the present choice of A rather than B; in fact, let the present enjoyment of B exclude the possibility of a future enjoyment of C. Finally, let us state the facts about quantity: B is a greater pleasure than either A or C taken singly, though the sum of A and C is greater than B. According to quantity as a criterion of preference, the student must admit that the rule of anyone's conduct in this case must be that he *should* prefer A and C to B. But, as a matter of fact, will everyone behave accordingly? To obtain the student's answer to this question, we take a concrete case in which the choice is between the pleasure of going to sleep as against the pleasure of further conviviality. Now the latter pleasure may be regarded as greater than the former taken by itself; but the former entails a future pleasure— the pleasure of feeling rested on the morrow, here set against the displeasure of weariness when there is work to be done. Let it even be supposed that the pleasure of feeling rested on the morrow, as now imagined, is less than the presently enjoyable pleasure of further carousing. It is only when the two pleasures—of sleep now and feeling rested tomorrow — are taken together, that they exceed the alternative which is involved. Will the student deny that a man who made such calculations as these might sometime violate the universal rule, and choose the lesser pleasure? The student will undoubtedly admit that he has made such a foolish choice himself; he will remember moments of repentance for having made the wrong choice, moments of resolution not to be so foolish again. But wherein lies the folly, unless it is wisdom to follow a true rule of conduct? And how could one ever repent, in cases of this sort, if the rule we have stated is strictly inviolable?

Shall we not, therefore, now ask the student to admit that by his own criterion of preference we have formulated a universally true rule of conduct, true for any man and yet also frequently violated? The student may still demur, saying that at the time of the choice, the lesser pleasure actually seemed the greater; and that repentance, with its recognition of folly, occurred at a later time when a more accurate calculation of the opposed pleasures was made. Thus, he may continue, it remains true as a matter of fact that men always prefer what at the time appears to them to be the greater pleasure, although the apparently greater may not be really so. Undoubtedly, we must admit, such mistakes in calculation are sometimes made, but that is not always the case. We can regret two sorts of mistakes: on the one hand, mistakes of calculation; on the other, mistakes of acting contrary to our calculations. It does not require much effort of thought to add to the pleasure of going to sleep now the con-

sequent pleasure of feeling refreshed in the morning; but it does require strength of will, as is popularly said, to give sufficient weight
to a future pleasure against a present one. That is why many men
have violated the sound rule which prescribes the choice of greater
pleasure (the sum of A and C, against B). At the moment of the
choice, they like B more than A, and even though they fully realize
that the alternatives do not consist of A against B, but of A, along
with C, against B, they foolishly put the morrow out of mind. They
set up as the maxim of their conduct, "Eat, drink, and be merry, for
tomorow we die." But if that maxim be a moral truth, then the rule
about always preferring the greater good must be false—on the condition, of course, that we do not die on the morrow. Since, as a
matter of fact, most of us make choices in the expectation of a normal
span of life, the maxim which permits us to take the greater pleasure
at the moment is false precisely because it is not the greater pleasure
in that larger framework of moments which constitutes a whole life.

We must ask the student at this point whether he is willing to
agree that a man, who has both memory of the past and imagination
of the future, exercises preferences not only for the present moment, but
for the future, and in view of his life as a whole. If he says No,
we need only remind him that he is neglecting obvious facts with which
he is acquainted, for example, the many cases in which he and other
men have preferred a momentary displeasure for the sake of a future
pleasure. As between going to the dentist now to have a cavity filled,
when the tooth is not yet decayed enough to hurt, and waiting for
toothache to set in, most of us make the choice of what is at the
moment unpleasant for the sake of avoiding a greater unpleasant-
ness later. If, in the light of cases of this sort, the student now
admits that the criteria of preference require us to consider future
moments as well as present ones, then we can formulate a principle
of preference, which subsumes the other two. This rule of conduct
is: In any case in which a choice can be made, men *should* prefer
the alternative, which, in the long run or viewing life as a whole,
maximizes pleasure and minimizes displeasure.

We must remind the student here that, so far, we have adopted his own criteria of preference,—pleasure against displeasure, or the greater quantity of pleasure,—and that we have succeeded in showing him, in terms of his own criteria, that he himself must acknowledge the truth of a moral rule, which is of universal application; and we have also now shown him that such a rule, especially in its most general formulation, is *normative*, saying how men *should* behave, not *descriptive*, saying how they *do*, the evidence for this being the obvious violations of the rule, and the experience of repentance for folly in so doing, whether it results from bad thinking or weak willing. In other words, the operations of men in exercising preferences cannot be simply instinctive, even though it be instinctive to man's animal nature to seek pleasure and avoid displeasure. We cannot ask *why* man *should* prefer pleasure to displeasure, for the student is right in replying that there is no reason for this except the fact of instinctive determination itself. But if in a complicated situation, involving sums of pleasure and displeasure, some present and some future, we ask *why* a man *should* prefer one set to another, instinct by itself will not suffice as an answer. Here it is necessary to say that, in view of man's instinctive preference for pleasure over displeasure, and in the light of memory and imagination, man has developed a rule of calculation which goes beyond the momentary promptings of instinct. Since this rule is not itself instinctive, it can be misapplied by bad thinking in particular cases, and even when the calculations are well performed, it can be violated by contrary choices. A violable rule of this kind, developed as the result of thinking about the problems of preference, can be called a rule of reason. It satisfies all the requirements of a universally true moral judgment, providing as it does both a prescription for conduct and a standard whereby to judge men's choices as wise or foolish, right or wrong. Hence we can say to the student that, accepting his own explanations of the fact of preference, we have removed one of the unqualified negatives in his moral skepticism, namely, that *no* universally valid moral judgment, no rule which directs all men everywhere, *is possible*. The possibility is more than proved by the existence of at least one such rule.

It is now the student's turn to remind us that we have another question to answer before we have really won our point. Granted that there is such a rule, it does not determine actual preferences in particular situations, for they are determined by the feelings of pleasure and displeasure, remembered, imagined, or presently experienced, which vary from individual to individual according to his temperament, his biographical conditioning, and his social environment. Hence, the rule that A should be preferred to B whenever A represents a greater plasure, is an empty formula, which does not oblige two men to agree in their actual judgments. One can say that he likes A better, and the other can say that he likes B better and so, without violating this so-called universal moral rule, the two men can make quite opposite choices in the same situation. Each man's preference expresses his own private opinion, and nothing more, for according to the rule itself, he has no grounds for saying that the other man has made a wrong choice. Certainly we must admit, the student tells us, that if moral judgments are worth anything at all, they must be practical: they must decide our conduct. Now the kind of judgments which decide our conduct are the actual judgments we make in particular cases, the judgment that *this* A is better than *this* B, here and now, and for me. The universal moral judgment that any A, which is a greater pleasure than any B, should be preferred, decides no one's conduct, for in particular situations, wherein we act, we do not find any A and any B, but this A and this B, and the whole question is whether we like this A better than this B. And although the universal judgment, that the greater pleasure should always be preferred to the less, is true for any man, the particular judgment that this pleasure is greater than that may be true only for me, and certainly need not be true for every man. Hence, the particular judgment, which must always carry the qualifying words "for me," is strictly an opinion, guiding only my own conduct, and if true in any sense at all, true only for me in this situation. But such particular judgments are the only ones which operate practically, and so, the student concludes, for all practical purposes moral questions are decided only by opinion. The moral skeptic is right, and the moralist wrong.

Much that the student has said is right, and yet his conclusion is wrong. Let us concede at once that, so far as our discussion has gone, all particular moral judgments, which express an individual's preference for A over B because more pleasing to him in the light of all calculable circumstances, are subjective, are opinions true for that individual only at the time they are made. Let us, furthermore, admit that such particular judgments are the most practical in the sense that they directly determine a choice and ensuing conduct. But instead of saying that they are the only really practical judgments, and that universal judgments are not practical at all, let us see if we can show the student that the universal judgments are also practical, though in a sense not so obviously or directly. Here are two men, facing the same alternatives under the same circumstances. The two men differ as individuals in many ways, and so whereas one likes this A better than this B, the other likes this B better than this A. Now suppose the situation to be complicated by the fact that both A and B involve future as well as present pleasures. What, then, does it mean to say that A is liked better than B, or B better than A? It must mean that each man, according to his individual nature, has made a different calculation here of which is the greater-good-for-him. But, as we have already seen, a man can act contrary to such a calculation, and in so doing violate the universal moral rule that the greater good should be chosen. Hence, there are the following possibilities: (1) if both men violate the universal moral rule, it can be truly said that each *should* have made the opposite choice; (2) if the first man obeys the universal rule, and the second transgresses it, then it can be said that the second man's judgment is wrong, even though it now will agree with the first man's. The first man's judgment is not right because this A in fact gives a greater pleasure than this B *to any man;* on the contrary, this B gives a greater pleasure to the second man; so that if the second man had acted wisely in his own behalf he *should* have chosen B rather than A.

What this all comes to can be summarized simply enough by pointing out that the act of preference follows from two judgments, not from one, a universal judgment and a particular judgment. With respect to the universal judgment, a man can be objectively right or wrong; thus, a man who says that a greater pleasure ought not to be preferred,—pleasure and the quantity of pleasure being the only criteria of preference,—speaks as falsely as a man who says two plus two does not equal four With respect to the particular judgment, a man can only be subjectively right or wrong, according as he correctly or incorrectly calculates what, for him in this situation, is the greater pleasure His being right in the particular judgment has no relevance to the choices of other men; whereas his being right in the universal judgment indicates what is right for every other man.

But, the student persists, how does the universal judgment have any practical bearing? The question can be answered in two ways. The first is difficult to imagine, though possible: the case of a man who actually was in error about the universal principle, who somehow thought that the greater pleasure ought not to be preferred. Such a man, however accurately he calculated his present and future pleasures in any particular situation, would, if he put his universal and his particular judgment together into practice, make a choice which could be called wrong—and objectively so, in the sense that it was not only wrong for him, but wrong for any man, because his error lay in an erroneous general principle. The second case is one we have already discussed: the case of the man who violates the true universal rule as a result either of wrong calculations in this particular situation, or as a result of not following the calculations according to the prescription of the universal rule. Whichever of these two things he does, his preference can also be objectively criticized. It was wrong not only for him, but for any man in the same situation. These facts indicate conclusively that having the right universal rule and, more than that, applying it accurately to the circumstances, and, even more than that, putting the combination of the universal and the particular judgments into practice, are indispensable conditions of reaching a sound conclusion in the particular case. And *any* man who fails to satisfy all of these conditions can be criticized objectively, as he could not be if the only factors which determined actual preferences were entirely subjective.

If that is so, the student then asks, why did you admit earlier in this discussion that one man can prefer this A to this B, and another prefer this B to this A, and both be quite right? Was not that

admission tantamount to conceding the subjectivity of actual preferences? Again, we must repeat that actual preferences, expressed in
the particular judgments which immediately precede action, are subjective in the sense indicated, namely, that two men can make opposite
judgments in the same situation and still both be right. The only
point the student failed to see, when he asked the question, was that
these opposite judgments are not *entirely* subjective, for both can be
wrong if both were reached in the wrong way, i. e., in reliance upon
a false universal rule, or in violation of a true one, through miscalcula-
tion or wilful transgression.

We have now arrived at a point favorable for summarizing our
discussion so far. Let us submit this summary to the student for his
approval before we go on.

There are two extreme errors which are equally wrong. (1) The
error of the moral skeptic who says that actual preferences are *entirely*
subjective, that there is absolutely no way of pointing out to a man
that he is wrong in a particular moral judgment in a manner which
would make any other man wrong in the same situation. (2) The
error of the moralist who says that actual preferences are *entirely*
objective, that there is absolutely no way in which a man can regard
his particular judgments as right for him and for himself alone,
since if they are right at all, they must be right for any other man
in the same situation. The truth, which corrects these errors, can
be succinctly summarized in the following propositions: (1) two
men can make opposite preferences in the same situation, and both
be wrong; (2) two men can make opposite preferences in the same
situation, and both be right. And if there is any moralist who makes
the error just described, the moral skeptic is thoroughly right in
attacking him. It may even be that the student has been led to
espouse moral skepticism because of the error he has attributed to
the moralist. Once the student is told that this error is no part of
the moralist's position, a stumbling block may be removed. So far as
we have gone, the moralist's attack upon skepticism can be justified
only with respect to the error that is a blemish on the skeptical position, just as much as the opposite extreme error is a blemish on the

position of the moralist. With both errors removed, the moralist and the moral skeptic are drawn a little closer.

With both errors removed, what can teacher and student (or moralist and moral skeptic) now positively agree upon? If they will examine together the two truths, stated above as corrections of the two extreme errors, they will find an explanation for these truths. On the one hand, the reason why two men can make opposite preferences in the same situation, and both be wrong, is that each can violate in his own way a rule that is equally obligatory on both. That there can be any universal moral truths at all, such as the rule for always preferring the greater pleasure, arises from the fact that, in so far as they are human, all men are the same, at any time or place. On the other hand, the reason why two men can make opposite preferences in the same situation, and both be right, is that both are not simply men, for each is a uniquely differing individual man, whose individual nature, constituted by the accidents of birth, biography, and environment, belongs to him alone. That two men, both adhering to the same universal moral rules and following them equally well, should be able to reach different conclusions arises from the fact that they differ as individuals; and the rightness of their opposite conclusions is a rightness relative to their individual natures. In short, whatever is universally true or objectively right in the making of a particular moral judgment is something relative to the human nature common to all men; whereas whatever is only individually true or only subjectively right in the making of such a judgment is something relative to the individual nature uniquely possessed by each man.

Now the moralist can claim to have moral knowledge, in the strict sense of objectively true moral principles or rules, only on the level of universal judgments. If he claims more than this, the moral skeptic is right in opposing him. The moral skeptic, on his side, can claim that moral judgments are subjectively true, or mere opinions, only on the level of particular judgments. If he claim more than this, the moralist is right in opposing him. The fact that the particular judgment is the one which is directly proximate to action does not mean that the universal judgment is not practical, for it is indirectly practical in so far as it is operative in the formation of the particular judgment. And although the particular judgment, taken as a whole, is subjective and has the status only of opinion, it contains implicitly the universal judgment which has been operative in its formation. It is necessary, of course, to extricate this universal judgment and to make it explicit, in order to discover a moral principle which has objective truth, obliging all men, and applicable to every situation.

There should be no difficulty about getting the student to approve this summary, for it says no more than what the student himself had admitted in the course of the preceding discussion. Making it, however, enables us to make two further points. The first looks backward. If the student, as a moral skeptic, still holds that although all moral standards are not individual, they are at least all conventional (relative to a social group at a given time and place), we can now begin to suggest to him that just as what is individual in moral judgments, because they are made by individual men, does not exclude the possibility of a universal element, because individual men are also all men, so what is conventional in moral judgments, because they are made by men living under certain social conditions, does not exclude the possibility of a universal element for the same reason, namely, that despite every difference of social origin, the men of different societies are still all men. We can promise the student to return to this point later, and show him, after a larger number of moral truths have been discovered, that these moral truths not only hold for every individual, but for every society as well; and that there is no inconsistency whatsoever between the unity and absoluteness of moral principles, on the one hand, and the plurality and relativity of *mores,* on the other.

The second point looks forward. It will be made by the student himself, after he has reviewed the ground we have so far covered. We have claimed, he will say, to have established the existence of moral theory, as a body of knowledge rather than a set of opinions, by getting him to admit the truth of one, or at most two, universal judgments, such as "men *ought* to prefer the greater pleasure." But if that is all that moral theory comes to, morality is not a very impressive body of knowledge. What other moral truths can we show him, and induce him to accept as such? If there are none other than this one, or its like, he does not regret his indifference to the study of moral philosophy, for at best it consists of the most obvious common sense, which all men already possess, and even at that its offering of acceptable truths is hardly elaborate enough to be worth more than a page, or the back of a card.

The challenge is utterly fair. We are now prepared to meet it. But, first, we must remind the student that we did not spend all this time on the principle, that men should prefer the greater pleasure, for its own sake, but rather for the sake of getting him to recognize a universal principle, a true but violable precept. And we had to do that in the student's own terms, by accepting at the outset his own answer to the question, Why is anything preferable to any other? He told us that the only criterion was pleasure as against displeasure; and then added a second criterion, the quantity of pleasure. At the time, we did not question these criteria. But now we can tell him that the paucity and obviousness of the principles we have so far reached are due to the two criteria of preference which he claimed were the only ones. Now that the first stage of the argument is completed, and he admits the existence of some universal truths, we can go further only if he will permit us to re-examine the original premises of the argument. They were not entirely wrong: pleasure and quantity of pleasure are criteria of preference. But, though not wrong, these criteria are inadequate. There are other and more fundamental criteria which, when seen, will not only bring us to the induction of much more significant moral generalizations, but also will significantly alter our understanding of the two criteria already discussed. In order to correct the error of supposing that the *only* criteria of preference are pleasure and quantity of pleasure, we must make a fresh start. The best way to do this is to re-examine some of the statements already made about pleasure, for in them much truth is contained that we have not yet seen.

CHAPTER III.

PLEASURE AND THE ORDER OF GOODS.

TO MAKE a fresh start, let us ask about the meaning of pleasure as a criterion of preference. Precisely what does the student mean when he says that he prefers A to B because A pleases and B displeases, or because A pleases him more than B?

The student may be somewhat bewildered by this question, for he has already told us that such judgments as "A pleases me more than B" are equivalent to saying "I like A more than B." In fact, he confesses, much of the discussion we have had so far has seemed to him to consist in making verbal substitutions of this sort. We started out by admitting that the fact of preference was equivalent to the judgment of "A-better-than-B-for-me" and that in turn became equivalent to two other forms of statement: "A pleases me more than B" and "I like A more than B." What has been gained by saying the same thing over and over again in different words? Pleasure and displeasure, it would seem, do not explain the fact of preference; far from explaining it, the fact of being pleased (or displeased) seems to be identical with the fact of preferring (or not preferring).

One thing the student says is false, but one thing is true. The falsity arises from his failure to remember that something was gained by introducing the notion of pleasure into our discussion. That, with the addition of considerations about quantity of pleasure, enabled us to formulate a universal rule of conduct, which he himself admitted *should* direct men's choices, though in fact men do not always choose as they should, according to this rule. This very discrepancy, between what *should be* and what *is,* certified the character of the rule we formulated as *moral* rather than *descriptive.*

The truth in the student's remarks was his observation that pleasure

31

does not explain preference. That is precisely why we are now engaged in re-examining the connection between preference and pleasure. And the first thing we must try to discover is whether pleasure is the object of every choice, or merely the result of every choice which is successfully executed. We say "every" here because pleasure does seem somehow involved in *every* act of preference. If pleasure results from getting what we prefer, then pleasure cannot be the cause of preference, since preference precedes execution, and we may not always be successful in getting what we have preferred. The student should be inclined to agree with the conception of pleasure as a resultant, since it was he who recently insisted that pleasure was not a cause.

Perhaps, says the student, but then I also return to my original insistence that there is no cause of preference. I only appear to explain my choice by speaking of pleasure, but preference is really inexplicable. And anyway, he adds, I don't see what difference it makes whether pleasure is the object of choice, as against displeasure, or the result of getting what I have chosen, as against displeasure as the result of failure. Why can't I say that I prefer something because I anticipate the pleasure I shall derive from getting what I want?

We must warn the student that in asking the last question he used the word "because" and thereby relaxed his resistance to our efforts at explaining preference. If he will stay relaxed for a moment longer, we may be able to get new light by following the lead of his last question. He must admit that making a choice precedes carrying it out in action, that deciding what one wants precedes getting it. Everyone knows, furthermore, that men do not always get what they want. Hence at the moment of choice, a man who has learned anything at all from experience must acknowledge the possibility of failure to possess what he has chosen. He must, therefore, anticipate the displeasure of failure as well as the pleasure of success. Even though men may be able to calculate the probabilities of success and failure in a particular case, and even though it is true that men sometimes avoid choosing a thing they really want because they wish to avoid the displeasure of likely failure in seeking what is a little beyond their present reach, pleasure and displeasure as anticipated resultants of successful or unsuccessful seeking are, at most, only one factor in the determination of every choice. The student was right in supposing that a man might prefer something *because* he anticipated the pleasure to be derived from getting what he wanted; but he was wrong if he supposed this to be the *only* cause, for it is now also evident that unless a man preferred this thing to that, he would not be pleased to get it, nor could he therefore anticipate the pleasure of successful seeking. The fundamental truth, which is slowly becoming apparent, is that the object of our preference is never the same as the satisfaction we experience in getting the object we prefer. Pleasure may be the object, or it may be the satisfaction, but it cannot be both without treacherous ambiguity in our use of words, and if it is not both there must be other factors than pleasure in the explanation of preference.

Or maybe preference cannot be explained, the student reminds us. But even if I waive that alternative to permit this discussion to go on, the student says indulgently, I am now at a loss to understand many points we have already agreed upon. Didn't we agree that A is preferred to B when A is pleasing and B displeasing, or when A is more pleasing than B? Doesn't that mean that A is a pleasure or a greater quantity of pleasure, and is not A the object of my choice when I prefer it, whether or not I succeed in getting it? If all this is so, then why can't I stick to my original statement that pleasure and displeasure, or unequal quantities of pleasure, are the only objects between which men choose when they exercise preferences?

The student's questions cannot be answered without begging him to be more attentive to words, for unless we now clarify our language we cannot accurately express our thought. At one moment, the student said "A is pleasing" and at another he said "A is a pleasure." Pointing this out to him, we must ask whether it makes no difference which we say. If he replies, as he is likely to, that he sees no difference here, we must try to explain, for upon the discernment of this difference much depends.

Let us begin by reminding the student that, at the very opening of our discussion when the fact of preference was first introduced, we pointed out that the only man who could say he never preferred anything would be a man who had never experienced desire of any sort.

And we said: if a man "admits having had the experience of desire, he can certainly be made to understand the difference between something which would satisfy that desire and something which would not. He can at least imagine a situation in which, given a certain desire, he would prefer one thing to another." Let us now call the thing he prefers the *object* of his desire. The object-of-desire is certainly not the same as the desire itself, nor is either of these the same as the satisfaction of the desire which occurs when the object is attained. There are three terms, then, which any careful analysis of preference must distinguish. They are irreducible to one another. And it is in the light of this fundamental distinction that the student can be made to see the difference between saying "A is a pleasure" and "A is pleasing." The latter statement means that A is pleasurable or a source of pleasure. The former statement means that A is itself identical with pleasure. But if A is both, then we are saying that that which is itself pleasure is a source of pleasure. If A is not both, then we must decide which A is, and upon this decision will depend whether we regard pleasure as the object of desire, or as the satisfaction which results from attaining the object of desire, for the object of desire is, when possessed, the source of satisfaction.

But, says the student, why cannot pleasure be both object and satisfaction? And even if we decided that pleasure was always one and not the other, what difference would it make?

The difference it would make is great. For if A is not itself a pleasure, and B a displeasure, then A and B as the objects between which preference is exercised must have some other determinate character. Let us suppose that A stands for wealth, or a course of action leading to its acquisition, and B stands for health, or a course of action leading to its preservation. Many men have been faced with these as alternatives to choose between. Let us further suppose that we use the words "pleasure" and "displeasure" to name the satisfaction and dissatisfaction of desire. Then the reason why, for a given man, wealth may be more pleasing than health, or conversely, is that he desires it more. We obviously cannot say that he desires it more *because it is more pleasing,* for unless he initially desired wealth more than health, he could not anticipate being pleased or satisfied if the course of action he pursued eventuated in its acquirement even at the expense of loss of health. Should we make the contrary supposition, however, that pleasure and displeasure are the objects of desire, rather than its satisfaction and dissatisfaction, then we can return to our original explanation of preference, namely, that we desire A more than B because A actually is a pleasure and B a displeasure, or because A is a greater pleasure than B. Here we do not say that A is a greater pleasure because we desire it more, but rather that we desire it more because it is a greater pleasure. The crucial question, in short, is whether desire is to be explained in terms of pleasure, or pleasure in terms of desire. If the latter is the case—and the student himself seems to have rejected the former in his earlier remarks about the failure to explain preference by identifying the preferred object with pleasure—then we must push further to explain why one object is desired more than another.

But, says the student, I still don't see why pleasure cannot be the object of desire, as well as its satisfaction. I see nothing wrong in saying that I desire or like pleasure and that pleasure pleases me. Before you go on to any further explanations, I'd like this point cleared up.

The student's insistence is justified, for there is a meaning of the word "pleasure" in which it does name *an* object of desire, and our whole problem here is to distinguish that meaning from another meaning of the word in which it names *every* satisfaction of desire. Once this basic ambiguity of the word "pleasure" is eliminated, and two quite distinct notions are distinctively expressed, we shall be able to proceed. It should be noted at once that "pleasure" cannot be used to name *every* object of desire, but only one sort of object among many others; in contrast, "pleasure" can be used to name every experience of satisfaction. As objects of desire, wealth and health are not the same as pleasure, although wealth and health can be pleasurable, i. e., they can be sources of pleasure in the sense that when possessed they satisfy the desire which led us to seek them. As pleasurable (i. e., pleasing, source of pleasure), pleasure as an object of desire is no different from health and wealth, for every object of desire is pleasurable. But to say that every object of desire is pleasurable in this sense is not to say that every object of desire is pleasure. If one were to say that pleasure is the only object of desire, one would be denying that such things as wealth and health are desirable objects.

This denial is not avoided by saying that wealth and health are desirable only because they are pleasurable, for, in the first place, that would apply to pleasure itself as an object of desire; and in the second place, it would amount to saying that an object of desire is desired *because* it will satisfy the desire when possessed. Since this applies to every object of desire, it cannot explain the preference for one over another; hence if wealth is preferred to health, it must be due to some difference between wealth and health as diverse objects of desire. Nor will quantity of pleasure help us here, for to say that we find wealth more pleasurable (i. e., a source of greater satisfaction) than health is to say no more than that we desire it or like it more; and we still have to explain *why we do* or *should,* in terms of something about the nature of these two objects, in themselves and in relation to ourselves.

Finally, pleasure itself as an object of desire is sometimes opposed to other objects, so that we are forced to choose between pleasure and other things. Thus, the man who seeks to gain great wealth must often forego pleasure, as the man who seeks certain pleasures often sacrifices his health in the process. In both these cases, pleasure can be regarded as an object of desire, competing with other objects which, as such, are simply not pleasure at all. Let A stand for pleasure as an object, B for wealth and C for health. Then to say, in the first instance, that a man prefers B to A is not to say that B is the greater pleasure, for it is not pleasure at all; it is rather to say that B will give him more pleasure, in the sense of more satisfaction, because he desires it more. Similarly, in the second instance, to say that A is preferred to C is to say that pleasure is more pleasurable than health, i. e., it will give greater satisfaction because it is more desired. And since to say that "pleasure is more pleasurable" is to say that "pleasure will give more pleasure" we are here plainly confronted with the ambiguity of the word "pleasure." It cannot mean the same thing when it names *one* object of desire (obviously *one,* since there must be some other object which gives less pleasure), and when it names *any* satisfaction (obviously *any,* since both objects give pleasure though in different degrees).

Not only is the ambiguity of the word "pleasure" thus revealed, but we can now help the student to understand what sort of *object* is named by "pleasure" when it is used in that meaning. Pleasure as an object of desire is a bodily condition, the opposite of which is the bodily condition known as pain. For want of better words, let us refer hereafter to sensual pleasure and sensual pain. Using words this way, we are certainly reporting the facts of human preference when we say that sensual pleasure is only one of the objects men desire, or that men often prefer other objects to sensual pleasure, or that some men actually prefer sensual pain because, under pathological conditions of desire, they derive greater pleasure from it. Furthermore, to call pleasure (as object-of-desire) sensual does not mean that pleasure (as satisfaction-of-desire) is inexperienceable. We experience satisfaction and dissatisfaction as states of desire itself, but not as directly sensed conditions of our body as a whole or of its members. A satisfied desire is experienced as one which no longer impels us to action; a dissatisfied one remains a motivating force. If the student finds this account of the two meanings of "pleasure" satisfactory, we can now return to the problem of preference and see how this clarification helps us.

The student will certainly concede that the ambiguity of the word "pleasure" has been sufficiently demonstrated, and he will probably admit that the suggested distinctions in meaning are genuine. He may even agree that the facts of human preference cannot be accurately *described* unless sensual pleasure (or sensual pain), as one among many objects of desire, is distinguished from what makes us regard either sensual pleasure or sensual pain as more or less pleasurable than other objects, namely, the strength of diverse desires and the resultant degrees of satisfaction to be obtained. And here the student makes one last effort to hold the position he once took—that pleasure, or quantity of pleasure, are the only explanations of preference. He tells us that he will use the word "pleasure" as equivalent to "satisfaction-of-desire," and using it this way, he claims that the general rule of conduct we have already formulated remains unaltered. That rule was: "In any case in which a choice can be made, men *should* prefer the alternative which, in the long run, or viewing life as a whole, maximizes pleasure and minimizes displeasure."

We must inform the student that it is not our intention to argue against the truth of this rule, but rather to criticize its insufficiency as a guide for human conduct. We must remind him that it was he who complained about the barrenness of moral knowledge if it went no further than this single universal rule. It was precisely in order to answer his complaint that we have been trying to show him that pleasure, taken in either of its senses, cannot account for preference. That being done, we may then be able to discover the real criteria which determine what a man should prefer, and in terms of these criteria formulate more specific rules of conduct. If the only rule of conduct were the one we have so far formulated, the student would be right, for the most part, in maintaining his moral relativism, and his skepticism about moral knowledge; different men might abide by this one rule and yet in every particular seek different things or make different choices. So far as this rule goes, it does not prevent us from supposing that one man could maximize pleasure by a set of actual choices quite different from those made by another man following the same rule; one man might always prefer wealth to sensual pleasure and honor, and another always prefer virtue to fame and fortune, and yet it would be conceivable that both could maximize pleasure in the sense of satisfying their differently oriented desires. When we say that pleasure is insufficient to explain preference, we mean, of course, not merely that it is insufficient to describe the fact of preference, but more fundamentally that, unless we go beyond pleasure, we can never say, of two objects different in kind, which *should* be preferred. Failing to do this, we fail to establish a practically significant body of moral rules, both universally valid and also violable.

If I understand you, says the student, you are at last agreeing with me. Pleasure being the only criterion, there is no moral knowledge worth bothering about, certainly no set of rules which would direct all men to follow the same general course of life. And I am now surer of this than I was before the discussion started. Distinguishing the two meanings of pleasure has helped to make it clear. For considering pleasure, in the first sense, as one object of desire, there appears to be no reason why men *should* concur in preferring it, or not preferring it, to other things. And considering pleasure, in the second sense, as equivalent to the satisfaction of every desire, all men *do in fact* concur in desiring as much satisfaction as they can get, but this fact does not obligate them to agree in preferring one sort of object to another. On the contrary, according as different men have different desires, it would seem as if they had to exercise quite different preferences in order to maximize pleasure in the sense of satisfaction.

Unless we can correct two errors which the student has made, we are barred from proceeding. The first may have been a slip of the tongue. The student spoke of "men desiring as much satisfaction as they can get." This statement seems to regard satisfaction as an object of desire, *which is strictly impossible*. If satisfaction were an object of desire, then satisfaction would result from fulfilling such desire, but the resultant satisfaction could not be the same as the satisfaction which, being desired and then possessed, gave rise to it. And there would be nothing to prevent the second satisfaction from being in turn an object of desire, thus giving rise to a third satisfaction in the same way, and so on in an endless progression. To make satisfaction an object of desire is, paradoxically, to condemn desire to endless dissatisfaction. Satisfaction, then, can never be an object of desire; nor can it ever explain why we desire one object rather than another, since given the desire for either object, its possession produces satisfaction.

The student's second error was his failure to note that our discussion has expanded to take in two new factors, namely, objects of desire other than sensual pleasure and pain, and a variety of desires of different strength. Pleasure is no longer the only criterion of preference; in fact, as object, it is only one among many things to be chosen; and as satisfaction, it is entirely insufficient as a criterion, since what will satisfy us depends upon our desires.

To make this clear, let us now introduce the word "good" to name any object of desire. The relation between *good* and *pleasure* is at once clear: sensual pleasure is a good, but not the only one; and every good is a source of pleasure in the sense of satisfying a desire when possessed. Hence, the earlier formula, that A is preferable to B whenever A is more pleasurable than B, must now be restated as follows: treating A and B as goods, both of which are desired, A is the greater good, and hence preferred, whenever the desire for A is greater than the desire for B. In short, the good is the desirable, and the better of two goods is the more desirable.

No, says the student, your last way of putting the matter is misleading. You have made it sound as if one object were in fact better than another, and your desire was determined accordingly; whereas so far as you have been able to show, one object is better than another only in so far as it is the object of a stronger desire. Thus you have not escaped the criterion of pleasure, since the preferred object, as the object of the stronger desire, is always the more pleasurable. Unless you can explain why all men should desire one object more strongly than another, you cannot avoid subjectivity and relativism. And how will you be able to show what men *should* desire and what they *should* prefer, unless you can show that the objects themselves are intrinsically good and bad, better and worse?

The student's challenge is fair. We have succeeded in showing him that pleasure will not explain either what men do prefer or what they should prefer, but we have not yet succeeded in establishing other criteria which are both adequate and objective. Some progress has been made, however, in so far as the student will now admit that there is a variety of goods, different in kind, where before he insisted that there was only one good, pleasure.

What do you mean by *a variety of goods?* the student interrupts, and whence comes this variety?

To answer these questions, let us examine the facts of life. For the moment we shall be content to enumerate the different sorts of objects which men do in fact desire. They desire food and drink, clothing and shelter. Each of these is *a kind* of good, just as sensual pleasure is *a kind* of good. We are here enumerating different *sorts* of objects which men in fact desire, and of each sort there are, of course, particular instances. Thus, "food" names a class of objects, including not only many subordinate varieties, but ultimately this or that partcular item of food—this slice of bread, that slab of butter.

But, the student interrupts again, how do you know whether a particular object belongs to one class or another? One man may desire this thing as *food,* and another desire it as *sensual pleasure.*

No, that is not so. Remember that sensual pleasure is a certain type of bodily condition. It is not the same, for instance, as another type of bodily condition which we call health. Now, food is neither sensual pleasure, nor is it health, but it may in fact be the cause of either, and hence, it may be desired as a *means* to the one or to the other. The student is quite right in anticipating the point that food (and, perhaps, also drink, clothing, shelter and all similar objects) are seldom desired for their own sake, but rather as means for obtaining other goods, other objects of desire, such as sensual pleasure and health. The fact that one kind of good is usually desired as a means for obtaining another kind of good does not obliterate the distinction between the two kinds; for if it did, we could never distinguish between objects desired as means and objects desired as ends.

Let us proceed with the enumeration, and make it briefer by naming more general classes of objects. The student has helped us to achieve this generality, for he has enabled us to see that all bodily goods (including strength and rest, as well as health and sensual pleasure) are of one large sort, just as food, drink, clothing, shelter and all similar things are of one large sort which we can call wealth. Wealth, it would appear, consists of all the physical things which men can use for the sake of their bodily well-being—for their health, sensual pleasure, etc. It includes everything the economist calls consumable goods and the instruments productive of them, and it includes money as an economic instrument involved in both the production and distribution of consumable goods. Now, in addition to such large classes of goods as wealth and bodily well-being, there are such things as friendship, social peace and security, public honor, political status, and perhaps also fame and power. In fact men do desire such things. Let us group them all together under the head of *social goods*.

Furthermore, some men, at least, seem to desire knowledge of various kinds and different sorts of skill. This group of goods resembles the bodily goods in one important respect: when a man possesses them he possesses them as an altered condition of his own nature, whereas the goods of wealth, in contrast, are all external goods, existing actually apart from man. But knowledge and skill do not exist actually apart from the men who possess them, and even if they be said to exist potentially, prior to actual possession, they exist potentially in men who have the capacity for developing them. It is difficult to find a name for this new class of goods. Despite their resemblance to bodily goods, they must be distinguished therefrom. The student would probably object to their traditional name—goods of the soul. Let us, therefore, call them *habits,* for the student will agree that skill in doing any sort of operation is an *acquired* habit. If the skill were native rather than acquired, it could not be an object of desire. Knowledge, like skill, is something we acquire, something we possess as a result of our own activity. Hence, for the time being, let us regard knowledge as a habit also. Certainly the student will admit that most men desire to be educated, and education is the process whereby men are helped to form habits of various sorts. The common desire for education can, therefore, be interpreted as the desire for a class of goods we have now grouped together as *habits.* If we ask why men want habits, such as knowledge and skill, the obvious answer is that they can act more efficiently as a result of possessing them. Hence, *efficient activity* must be still another kind of good, since whenever one kind of good is desired for the sake of another, the latter must also be regarded as a kind of good.

Without claiming that this enumeration is either precise or exhaustive, we can now ask the student whether he will accept the five types of goods we have named (viz., wealth, bodily goods, social goods, habits, activity) as a rough indication of the variety of goods which men do in fact desire.

Yes, says the student, men do in fact seem to desire all these objects, and I will admit that it is possible to divide them into the groups you have named. But I am not sure I understand why there is this variety of goods; or to put my question another way, is there any reason why this variety is the same for *all* men? Unless it is, you are not going to be able to show that all men *should* exercise the same preferences in choosing among goods of these various sorts. And even if it is, an objective ordering of these goods still remains to be shown, for men do in fact seem to make quite different choices—some men desire health and knowledge for the sake of wealth and power; others desire wealth for the sake of sensual pleasure and fame; and there may even be some who desire wealth and the social goods for the sake of habits and efficient activity.

One thing at a time. Let us first explain to the student why some such variety of goods is the same for all men. The first part of the answer should be obvious at once. As men, having human nature, all men are the same, even though they differ in many subordinate ways as individuals. The deeper question, however, is why there is a variety of goods, not why it is the same for all men. If the good is simply any object—whether an external thing or an aspect of human nature itself—which a man desires, then the plurality of diverse objects, which we have classified as a variety of goods, must be due to a plurality of diverse desires. What the student really wants to know is why all men *should* have the same set of desires. We cannot rely upon the fact that all men *do* have the same plurality of desires, for the fact may be questionable, and even if it is not, the student is justified in asking why he, for one, should not make an exception of himself and limit his desires to fewer objects. If there is no reason why he should not do this, then regardless of the facts about what most men desire, the variety of goods is a subjective, not an objective, enumeration. There is a further crucial consequence: the objects we have called goods are good *only because they are desired*. Hence there is always a relativity of the good to actual desire, and we shall never be able to say what men *should* desire, which is central to moral knowledge as normative or pre-scriptive. In order to get beyond a mere description of what men *do* desire, we must somehow show the student that the objects men desire, they desire *because they judge them to be good*. Paradoxical though it seem, we must begin to do this by getting the student to admit one fact: *all men desire to live*.

Yes, says the student, I'll admit that fact. Even if there were exceptions, it would certainly be true that a man who does not desire to live desires nothing else, and for him there is no further problem.

Will you admit one further thing? we must ask. Will you admit that all men desire to live well, or as well as possible?

Yes again, says the student, although I am not sure I know what is meant by "living well" nor do I think that all men would agree about what living well consisted in. I'll say Yes, therefore, if all you mean is that every man wants as much satisfaction as he can get. To say this is to say no more than what we have already agreed upon—that every man wishes to maximize pleasure, or, in our new terms, every man seeks the utmost satisfaction of which he is capable.

In saying this, the student has helped us to our conclusion. Though perhaps inadvertently, he has introduced an indispensable notion, that of human capacity. If living well consists in fulfilling a man's capacities, (and in so far as these capacities are the same for all men because they are rooted in a common human nature), then it follows that whatever objects are necessary to accomplish such fulfillment must be desired by any man who desires to live well. And such objects are no longer to be called good simply because they are in fact desired; we can now see that they are good because it is necessary to desire them if one desires to live well. We can say a man should desire whatever is necessary for achieving what he does in fact desire—namely, a good life. And the objects he should desire, as means to the end he does desire, are good, not because he does desire them, but because they are means to the desired end. If the end is living well, we can say that the five kinds of good we have named are all objectively good because they are indispensable means. A man should desire them if he seeks to live well; if in fact he does not, he is clearly in error. That men can make such errors, for one cause or another, indicates the violability of this prescription and verifies its character as a moral rule, a rule as universal as the commonness of the desire for a good life, and the commonness of human nature as the root of certain capacities to be fulfilled.

We need not pause here to show in detail how the variety of goods enumerated corresponds to the diversity of capacities to be realized. In general, it should be clear that living consists in activity, that the capacity for activity is more fully realized according as we are able to act more efficiently, that habits are the immediate conditions of such efficiency, that bodily and social goods are its remote conditions, and that wealth is indispensable to the maintenance of bodily well-being. Or, to put it another way, we have capacities for health and sensual pleasure, for social and intellectual activity, for work and play—and the variety of objects enumerated corresponds to these capacities. They are good for this reason, and we should desire them accordingly. In short, the student now has the answer to the question, whence comes the variety of goods? It comes from the variety of capacities which men can fulfill, and which they should fulfill in order to live well.

I may have helped you make all these points by mentioning *capacity*, the student says, but you have gone much further than I can follow. I am not quarrelling with your point of view that, in general, human capacities are the same—so far as they are rooted in a human nature which is the same. But, remember, I did not agree that all men meant the same thing by such words as "living well." Even if the variety of goods is the same for all men in some sense, the fact remains that different men place different values on the various goods; and although you may have shown that all men *should* desire them, you have not shown that all men *should* concur in desiring them in the same way—with the same emphasis, to the same extent, in the same order. And you must show this, since you have to admit the contrary facts—namely, that men do in fact differ in the way they exercise desire with respect to the same variety of goods. My guess is that they differ because they mean quite different things when they all admit they want to live well. Furthermore, if the various goods we have been talking about are objects we *should* desire because they are indispensable *means* to the end we *do* desire, they why *should* we desire the *end* itself? If you tell me that there is no point to this question, and we can rest in the fact that we do desire something as an end, then I say, in terms of all your reasoning so far, that the end is not desired because it is good, but rather good only because it is desired. Unless you can show it is good apart from being actually desired, you cannot show that men *should* desire it.

The student has accurately indicated what remains to be seen. Though there is some ground yet to be covered, we have come a long way from the initial suppositions of our discussion. Let us summarize the advances we have made: (1) we agree that pleasure does not, in either of its two senses, explain the fact or justify the exercise of preference; (2) we agree that an object is good when it is desirable, not simply when it is actually desired, and that it is desirable as somehow related to the fulfillment of human capacities; (3) we agree that there is a variety of such desirables, i. e., goods which *should* be desired by all men, because they are indispensable as means to an end all men do in fact desire, namely, to live well; (4) we agree that this variety some-how corresponds to the variety of capacities common to human nature, and that the diversity among our desires is determined by the diversity of desirables, or goods. In terms of all this, we have been able to formulate a universal (and quite violable) moral rule: all men *should* desire every sort of good which is an indispensable means to a desired end. But, as the student rightly points out, three questions remain. (1) Why *should* any end be desired, simply as an end and not as a means? (2) Why *should* all men desire the same end, not only verbally named in the same way, by such a phrase as "living well," but really understood in the same way. (3) Why *should* all men desire the means (consisting of whatever kinds of goods should be desired for the sake of the end) in the same way—i.e., in the same order, with the same emphasis upon each kind, etc.?

Since anything which is desired must be desired either as a means or as an end or as both, our analysis of goods or desirables will be complete—if only in a general way—when we succeed in answering these three questions, for then we will know why anything at all *should* be desired, either in itself or in relation to something else. And since the problem of preference is concerned with the reasons for choosing between one sort of good and another, as alternative means to some end, the problem will be completely solved when we know the *order* of all the goods which are means to an end which should be the end all men seek.

The first question to answer is the one about the end. Beginning with the fact of preference, our discussion began with a consideration of means—alternative goods between which choice must be exercised. But now we see that we cannot solve the problem of any preference unless we first solve the problem of the ultimate criterion of all preferences, namely, the end, which is itself never preferred, because it is not *a* good, opposed by alternative goods, but *the* good, having no alternatives. It is necessary, therefore, to make another fresh start.

CHAPTER IV.

THE ORDER OF GOODS AND HAPPINESS.

W E MUST NOW BEGIN by asking the student whether he is willing to agree that we cannot desire everything as a means. Some things we may desire simply as means, and some as ends which are in turn means to further ends, but must we not desire at least one thing simply as an end, and in no sense as a means?

I suppose so, the student will probably say, but I don't see why.

The reason is not hard to find. You admit that whatever is desired as a means is sought for the sake of its end, and unless the end is desired, whatever may be a means to it is not desirable. Now although an end is the last thing we actually achieve in the course of our conduct (for if an end could be achieved before some of its means, those means would be utterly dispensable), the end must be the first thing we actually desire, for unless we desire the end, we have no reason for desiring things which are good only as means to it. Hence if every good which we regard as an end could also be regarded as a means to some further end, and so on indefinitely, there would be no beginning. Just as you cannot begin to walk in a definite direction unless you know where you are going before you start, so you cannot desire anything at all as a means unless you desire something simply as an end.

Granted, says the student, something must be desired as an end. But you seem to be implying that there is only one end for each man, and the same for every man. Why cannot a man have several distinct ends? And why cannot different men have different ends?

Let us first consider the problem of several distinct ends for a single man. Suppose A and B to represent two objects, each of which is desired for its own sake, simply as an end. Now either the man seeks both ends together, as parts of a whole we shall call X, or he chooses between them. But if he chooses between them, he is exercising preference. And he must exercise this preference before he desires any other goods which are means either to A or to B, for until his end is determined, he cannot select the means. But on what ground shall he choose between A and B as ends? Since neither is a means, he cannot decide between them as he might be able to decide between alternative means to the same end. Therefore, if he prefers one end to another, he must do so because—because—

Because he likes it more, the student answers, and we are right back to where we started. The preference for A over B (now called ends) must be made as I originally said every preference was made—in terms of a man's likes and dislikes, in terms of the quantity of pleasure to be obtained. Or, if you want me to avoid such words as "pleasure," I'll say that the man will choose the end which satisfies him most.

It only *seems* as if we have fallen back; on the contrary, we have made a great advance. Let us show this to the student by asking him whether if a man could get *some* satisfaction out of having A, and *some* also out of having B, would he not get more satisfaction out of having X, consisting in the sum of A and B. In which case, if the criterion which determines a "choice of ends" (in our supposititious case) is the amount of satisfaction to be derived from possessing it, then whatever gives the utmost satisfaction should always be chosen. And if, again in our supposititious case, A and B are the only two possibilities as ends, then neither can really be the end, for the end must be X, the whole which includes them as parts. If a man seeks either A or B when he can seek X, he is seeking less satisfaction than he can have. And even though A and B are ends, they must also be regarded as means: the parts of a whole are means for getting the whole itself. Therefore, there is only one thing which is the end for any man. It is always the totality of all the goods he is capable of possessing, and possessing each derives *some* satisfaction therefrom. Complete satisfaction occurs only when the totality is somehow possessed. The end, therefore, is always the whole of goods; the parts of this whole are the different kinds of goods, each of which as a part is a *constitutive* means to the whole—constitutive in the sense that it is a means whereby the whole can be constituted. The constitutive means, or we can call them partial goods, may be related to *one another* as means are to ends, but all of them, in so far as they are parts, are equally constitutive means with respect to the whole. That is why A and B as partial goods may be ends in relation to other partial goods (C and D, let us say) serving them as means. But in so far as they are partial goods, neither A nor B can be *the* end, and both together, along with C and D, and all other partial goods, must be regarded as constitutive means with respect to X, which now stands for the complete totality of goods or desirables. Hence there is always only one real and ultimate end, never desired as a means, and since there is only one, it can never be the object of choice or preference. It *must* be desired, because there is no alternative to it.

You are going too fast for me, the student confesses. I am particularly bothered by two things. One is that you seem to be assuming that all the partial goods are always compatible with one another, so that it is always possible for a man to have all of them. The other is that you seem to be reverting to an earlier position, or even worse than that, you seem to be saying the opposite of what you said before. You said before that satisfaction cannot be an object of desire, and yet now you seem to be saying that X must be taken as the end, rather than A or B, because it is more satisfying than they are. Furthermore, if the totality of goods *is* always *the* end, then it is silly to say that a man *should* seek to achieve this totality, since he cannot seek otherwise. In fact, I don't see that we are saying now any more than we said before when we said that a man should seek to maximize pleasure, or satisfaction—only it now appears there is no *should* about it.

Let us meet the student's first point by reminding him how the diversity of partial goods is generated. There are many different kinds of good because man has different capacities to be fulfilled. Now, of course, it is possible for human capacities to be so related that any attempt to fulfill one would necessarily interfere with the fulfillment of one or more of the others. But that, as a matter of fact, does not seem to be the case. In the light of the facts about human nature, we can say, then, that so long as the variety of goods corresponds somehow to the diversity in human capacities, this variety will include no incompatible partial goods. Hence, a variety so constituted can always be summated in a totality. If A, B, C, D .... N represents an exhaustive enumeration of partial goods, each can be a part of the totality, X, for they can be taken together as means to constitute that whole.

Before we leave this point, we can clarify another related matter. The student will recall that in the concrete cases of preference which we considered earlier, the need for choice arose from the fact that the alternatives were exclusive of one another. That always is the case when we are faced with particular instances of the same sort of good —this particular way of getting sensual pleasure, for example, as opposed to that. It is precisely in such cases, that the criterion of quantity becomes operative—in fact, is indispensable. As between competing particular goods of essentially the same sort, a man should choose the greater—assuming, of course, that it is right for him, all else being considered, to choose that sort of good at all. But when the choice is between particular goods essentially different in kind, the criterion of quantity no longer operates in the same way. In the first place, different kinds of good cannot be compared with respect to quantity, for each yields a different kind of satisfaction, in whatever amount that may be. In the second place, different kinds of good are not competing but completing—if we have been right in saying that each kind in a correctly enumerated variety of goods is as indispensable as every other kind. This does not mean that we are never forced to choose between particular goods of different kinds; it means rather that the criterion of quantity now operates only with respect to the end—the totality— and in view of that end, we must make this particular choice here and now in such a way that we can ultimately obtain every kind of good, even though at this moment we do that by giving up one particular good for a particular good of another kind. The totality of goods is achieved not by possessing *every particular good,* but goods of *every kind*. We shall return to this point later in discussing the order of goods.

Let us now consider the student's second point. He is right in noticing a reversion to an earlier stage of our discussion, and even in detecting an apparent contradiction of what was said before. We said that the satisfaction derived from possessing a particular desirable object (a particular instance of a kind of good) could not be the object of that desire, for then the satisfaction, not the object itself, would be desirable. Nor can it be said that the object is desirable only for the sake of the satisfaction to be derived, for, in the first place, that generates an infinite regress of objects of desire; and, in the second place, we have seen that a choice between two sorts of objects cannot be explained or justified in this way. It should be noted, therefore, that this earlier point was not relevant to the problem of preference in so far as it involved two kinds of goods as the alternatives. But we have now seen that the amount of satisfaction, without becoming the object of desire, can operate as *a* criterion (though, perhaps, not the only criterion) in choosing between two particular instances of the same sort of good. And when we come to the question of the ultimate end, at which point there is no problem of preference at all, the "amount" of satisfaction, now understood hetergeneously, rather than homogeneously, as includ-ing every kind of satisfaction, properly becomes the only criterion. Since we have used the word "criterion" to mean that by which we judge in our acts of choice or preference, it might be better to say that the amount of satisfaction is the *sign,* rather than the criterion, of the ultimate end, which is the totality of goods. The end should be that which leaves nothing to be desired. The end, in a sense, puts an end to desire by the completeness of the satisfaction which results from posses-sing, not every particular good, which is impossible, but every kind of good, which is quite possible.

It may be worth while to try to say this in another way. The end can be described by the words "all good things," which must be under-stood to mean a totality of kinds of goods, not all the particular goods in each kind. The end, as a totality of goods, cannot itself be regarded as *a* good, for then the whole would belong to itself as a part. If we refer to the end, thus conceived, as an object of desire—and it can be an object of desire, though not of choice or preference—we must refer to it as *the* good. And for every man there can be only one object of desire which is *the* good, though there are many objects of desire, subject to choice or preference, which are particular instances of goods, either of the same kind or of different kinds. So far we have spoken of goods objectively—as objects of desire. Now we can say the same thing subjectively, in terms of the satisfaction of desire. Satisfaction results from the possession of any object of desire, but the peculiar subjective *sign* of the object which is *the* good is that satisfaction is complete when it is possessed. Because of the peculiar relation between the end objectively conceived as an heterogeneous totality of kinds of good, and the end subjectively realized as an heterogeneous sum of satisfactions, we can always speak of the end subjectively as well as objectively. We cannot do this in the case of any partial good, for unless we name the *kind* of object desired, we cannot know the *kind* of satisfaction derived. But if one were to say that the end of all desire is "complete satisfaction," one would know this to be the subjective counterpart of that unique object of desire which consists in "all good things."

The student was wrong in thinking that we had become involved in a contradiction, but he was right in noticing that our present discussion of the end gives new significance to our earlier discussion of pleasure. When we are concerned with objects of desire—alternatives for preference—pleasure is not the only good; nor is it ever the sufficient criterion for determining a choice between particular objects. But when the maxim concerning the desirability of the greatest quantity of pleasure is properly understood in terms of the sum of satisfactions, that maxim directs us to the end of all our desires—a totality of diverse goods. To say that every man wants as much pleasure as possible is to say that every man wants a good life—a life enriched by every sort of good. In short, the end must be so conceived that if it could be obtained by one decision, no man could resist making this decision, no man could choose or prefer anything else because, by the very nature of the case, everything else must be less good. And the end we have now envisaged meets that test, whether we think of it as a totality of diverse goods or as the utmost in pleasure, the complete satisfaction of desire.

I am still not sure I understand what you are driving at, says the student. For one thing, what makes you think it is possible for a man to get all good things? Every man may want as much pleasure as possible, but unless as much as possible can really be obtained, I don't see that the end you have envisaged is any better than the pot of gold at the end of the rainbow. You'll have to show the man from Missouri how he can get all good things. And, in the second place, the rule which directs a man to seek the end, as you have defined it, no longer seems to be a *moral* rule by your own criterion, for it is obviously inviolable. A man could not seek anything else. You have really admitted what I have always suspected—that it is a *natural* law, not a *moral* law, of human nature, for men to try to get as much as they can. You have simply described human behavior, and so far as I can see it is no different from animal behavior.

Let us begin with the student's second point. But before we do that, there is one other point to be made. The student previously asked us to show that the end is the same for all men. We have so far only succeeded in showing that for a given man there is just one end, because the end is never *a* good, but always *the* good. But when *the* good is conceived as a totality of diverse goods, including every sort of desirable object, is it not clear at once that *the* good must be the same for every man? The reasoning here is simple: all men have the same human nature; hence they have the same set of capacities to be fulfilled, however much they may differ individually in the degree to which they possess this or that capacity; hence for every man the variety of objects which can fulfill these capacities and satisfy the plurality of human desires will include the same diversity of kinds of good; therefore, the end, conceived as *all good things* (and understood as an heterogeneous totality of goods or satisfactions, not of course, as an undifferentiated maximum quantity) must be the same for all men.

The reasoning is all right, says the student. It should have been obvious to me, I suppose, that if you could prove there is only one end for each man, you could also show that the end is the same for every man, for in both cases the reasoning depends on human nature. But the joke is on you, because you have now strengthened my point that the end as you have defined it simply *describes* what *in fact* every man seeks. If there is any truth in what you have been saying, it is a psycho-

logical truth, not a moral truth. Remember that you yourself told me
that a moral rule had to be violable. Well, if you were to phrase a rule
about the end—such as, *Seek all good things*—it couldn't be violated.

It may be appropriate at this juncture to tell the student that, in the
tradition of moral science, the rule about the end is regarded as the first
principle of morality. Whether it be expressed by such words as "Seek
all good things" or even more simply by "Seek *the* good," this rule is
said to be the first precept of the natural moral law. The student should
now be able to see why the first principle of moral knowledge must be
a rule about the end, since he has come to realize that every object
which is not *the* good, but only *a* good, is good only as a means, and
hence good in terms of the end. He has realized, though perhaps
vaguely, that only by reference to the end can a choice between means
be determined. That is why the end is the first principle, without which
the problem of preference cannot be solved. How that problem is solved
remains to be seen, but first we must meet the student's objection to
the rule about the end—not as a *natural* law, but as a *moral* principle.

Some time back the student admitted that all men desire to live.
(Those who do not have no moral problems!) He was even willing to
say that all men desire to live well, though he added the qualification
that what one man meant by "living well" might differ considerably
from what another meant. He should now be prepared, however, to
relax that qualification somewhat; for if the words "living well" name
the end which all men seek, and be understood as equivalent to "a life
enriched by the possession of all good things," then it would appear that,
in one sense at least, all men must agree about what they mean by "living
well." Let us call the sense in which all men agree about the end a *formal
conception* of it. All men subscribe to the same formula: a totality of
diverse goods, a maximum of diverse satisfactions. But the student would
be quite right in insisting that, though men may not differ about this
formula, they appear to differ considerably about how they interpret it.
Far from disputing the student on this point, we, too, insist upon it, because herein lies the clue to the *violable,* hence *moral,* character of the
first principle—the rule about the end.

To carry the analysis further, it might prove useful here to introduce a new term—*happiness*. The way in which men ordinarily use the word "happiness" justifies us in identifying happiness with the end. They regard happiness as something desirable entirely for its own sake. No one would ever speak of wanting happiness for the sake of obtaining some further or other good. The happy man is one who wants for nothing more. Hence it is clear that happiness is not *a* good; it is not even accurate to speak of it as "the highest good" if such words signify that happiness is one good among others, albeit the greatest. Happiness is the same as what we have called *the* good, the supreme good; but it is *summum bonum* only in the sense of being the totality or sum of every kind of good. Furthermore, we can identify happiness with living well, or with a good human life, since the formula is the same in both cases. The relation between happiness and pleasure is also clear: surely happiness is not the same as sensual pleasure, which is merely one kind of good; nor is happiness, considered objectively, the same as pleasure in the sense of satisfaction; but when we consider happiness, or the end, subjectively, it can be understood in terms of pleasure, for in possessing all good things the happy man enjoys every sort of satisfaction and in this sense has maximized pleasure.

That all men desire happiness seems to be the law of their nature. Though this be true, we also know as a matter of fact that men lead different sorts of lives. If we examine the matter closely, we find that there are great differences in the accounts they give of happiness—of what they are seeking, of what they are trying to get out of life. What is the source of these differences? Since the formula of happiness is the same for all—a whole of diverse goods, a sum of diverse satisfactions— there are only two ways in which men can differ in putting matter into the formula, i.e., in passing from a *formal* to a *material* conception of their end, or happiness. (1) They can differ in their enumeration of the kinds of goods. (2) They can differ in the way they order whatever goods they have enumerated; by "order" here is meant an estimation of the relative worth of the various sorts of goods—some of which *should be preferred* to others, some of which, within the plurality of goods itself, are related to others as means are to ends. Now according as men differ in either of these ways, or both together, the happiness they seek will be differently constituted, for happiness as a totality of goods is a whole constituted by the variety and order of its parts. Will the student now agree that we have described the facts which he had in mind when he said that though all men may seek the same end (to live well, happiness), they do not seek the same thing? Will he permit us to express this truth more precisely—and less paradoxically —by saying that the end all men seek is the same *formally*, but different *materially?*

Yes, says the student, your language says what I mean. But I don't see how this is going to show the natural law of human behavior to be a moral rule—a rule (about the end) which is violable.

We are now prepared to show the student that. Only one new point needs to be added. Considered materially, there are many different conceptions of happiness. The differences are, for the most part, with respect to the order of goods—one man emphasizing wealth, let us say, another friendship, another knowledge, and so forth. There may be differences in the listing of the goods; though this is less frequently the case, some men have omitted sensual pleasure as a good, others have omitted the social goods, and some have even omitted knowledge and what has been called "moral virtue." Now the new point we must add (and prove) is simply this: that among all the different conceptions of happiness which men have recorded, there is only one right conception, in material detail, of the variety and order of goods. If a man seeks anything other than happiness as rightly constituted, he is not really seeking happiness at all, but a false or illusory version of it, even though the wrong thing he seeks he seeks as his ultimate end because he conceives it under the same formula. Let us call the end as rightly conceived the *real* good; let us call the end as wrongly conceived the *apparent* good. Using words this way, we can see that if the rule about the end is expressed by "Seek the good, real *or* apparent," then it cannot be violated, for it is simply a natural law, a description of how man must in fact behave—and being a *description* it is incorrectly expressed as a *prescription*, in the imperative mood rather than the declarative. But if the rule is expressed by "Seek the *real* good," then it is violated by every man who wrongly conceives his end, and we have a moral law, truly prescriptive, saying what men *should* seek. The same thing can be said in terms of happiness: "Seek happiness properly constituted by a correct enumeration and a right ordering of goods" can be violated in many ways; but "Seek happiness as *any* collection of goods in *any* order" cannot be violated at all. In short, if *materially* there is one right, and many wrong, conceptions of happiness, the fact that all men seek the same end formally does not mean there is no violable rule about the end. On the contrary, there is a rule the violation of which leads away from rather than toward real happiness.

IF, says the student, *if.* Everything seems to depend now upon your hypothesis that men can be mistaken about how their happiness is constituted. The hypothesis being granted, I can see that much will follow. Those who have mistaken notions about what their happiness really consists in will probably not do what they *should* do in order to live well or become happy. But why should I grant your hypothesis?

The student is right to raise this question. Once he affirms the hypothesis, he ceases to be a skeptic or a relativist about morals, for every other moral truth can, in a way, be drawn from a true conception of the end. The student's question has, however, already been answered. Though perhaps he did not realize it at the time, he affirmed the hypothesis when he agreed to the reasoning by which we proved, in terms of every man's having the same capacities, rooted in the same human nature, that "the variety of objects which can fulfill these capacities and satisfy the plurality of human desires will include the same diversity of kinds of good" *for every man.* The truth about happiness is thus seen to follow from the truth about human nature, and that is why the first principle of conduct (the rule about the end) is not only moral, because violable, but also natural. It is not only natural for men everywhere and at all times to seek *all good things,* but it is also in terms of their nature that the variety and order of goods constituting this whole *should be the same for all.* Men cannot act contrary to their nature in wanting to be dissatisfied, or, if you will, in wanting less than complete satisfaction. But they can make mistakes in understanding their nature, and as a result of such mistakes set up a wrong conception of happiness which, if followed, must ultimately lead them to frustration—the achievement of less than is possible to their nature.

Thus, for example, if a man make the error of supposing no essential difference to exist between human nature and that of brute animals, and if, accordingly, he conceive himself as having no capacities beyond those possessed by brutes, he will misconceive human happiness by omitting from its constitution those distinctively human goods which fulfill capacities which man alone has. His error here may not be one of simple omission; it may take the form of misunderstanding the distinctive character of the specifically human goods. However the error is made, the result will be the same. A man cannot become happy by trying to live a good animal life. He must try to live a good human life. In a manner of speaking, one can say that animals seek "happiness' in so far as they, too, live according to natural law. According to the law of their nature, there is a sum of goods which can fulfill their capacities, a totality which they are driven instinctively to seek. But there are two profoundly significant differences between the natural law which governs animal and that which governs human conduct. One we have already seen—the difference in what is the sum of goods for each according to its nature. The other is that, in detail as well as generally, animal seeking is instinctively determined, and hence there can be no discrepancy between what animals *do* seek and what they *should* seek; whereas human seeking is "instinctively" determined only with respect to the end as formally conceived; hence men may in fact not seek what they should. This is just another way of saying that men, unlike brute animals, are able to think about their end, and since wherever thinking occurs, error may happen, men can misconceive their happiness. Unable to think abstractly, animals cannot conceive, and hence cannot misconceive, their end. Therefore, there is only a natural law, but no moral law, of animal behavior, whereas human conduct is susceptible of direction by a *natural moral* law.

I have gradually come to realize, the student confesses, how important a role the conception of human nature plays in the discovery of universal moral principles. But it never occurred to me before that I had to swallow all this stuff about the *essential* difference between men and animals. All the psychology I have studied—experimental psychology, animal psychology—as well as all the biology, and especially the business about evolution, is against such a notion. If this new point is indispensable to the argument, you've got a lot more proving to do. For the moment I don't see that it is indispensable, and so I'll waive the point in order to ask another question. I'll grant that all men have the same human nature—whether or not that is essentially different from the nature of animals. I can see how, in terms of that common nature, happiness must be really the same for all men, in the sense of including the same variety of goods; and I can also see that, if men misconceive their nature, they will probably misconceive what is really good for them. But you pointed out before that men misconceive happiness in two ways—both with respect to the variety of parts which constitute the whole of goods, and also with respect to the ordering of these parts. Moreover, you said that the most frequent errors occur with respect to the ordering of the partial goods, rather than in their enumeration. This requires some explanation. I don't see why there need be any ordering of goods. If a man rightly enumerate the parts of happiness, why cannot he get the whole by going after the parts in any order?

To answer this very difficult question, let us begin by reminding the student that, at an earlier point, he wondered whether it is *possible* for a man to get *all good things*. He compared the end, thus envisaged, to the rainbow's end. He wanted to be shown just *how* a man can get all good things. Now, in the first place, let us remember that *all good things* does not mean *every* particular good, but only *some of every kind of good*. If this were not so, it would take an infinitely long life to get all good things, and, furthermore, the pursuit of happiness would be competitive—as is the attempt to corner the market and possess every piece of a certain commodity. But this is not the case; however much in fact they do, men *need not* interfere with one another in the pursuit of happiness. In the second place, let us remember that *all good things* is a possible whole because the various kinds of good which are its parts do not exclude one another. They are all *compossible* with one another; if they were not, the whole we have supposed to be constituted by them would be self-contradictory and impossible. In the third place, there is a new consideration, the point about order. Either the order in which we go after the various partial goods makes no difference, or it does. Suppose it makes no difference. Then happiness would be easily achieved by anyone who made a right enumeration of the partial goods. Regardless of whether such a man subordinated wealth to knowledge, or knowledge to wealth, regardless of whether he spent a great deal of his time and effort in search of sensual pleasures or postponed taking care of his health until after he had achieved public honor, he would not be prevented from becoming happy *so long as he included every sort of good among the objects of his pursuit.* But this appears to be contrary to the facts of life as we know them. The familiar saying that "there can be too much of *a* good thing" applies to some of the partial goods which enter into the constitution of happiness: too much of some of them can disbar us entirely from others. Not only must the degree to which we seek certain types of good be proportioned to their worth as parts of the whole, in order to prevent them from interfering with our possession of other types, but each kind of good must be seen in its functional relation to every other kind, according to the functional interdependence of the capacities of human nature, which these different kinds of objects are able to fulfill. We must conclude, therefore, that a man cannot become happy unless, in seeking *all good things,* he does so in the right order and with due proportion. That is why happiness is difficult to achieve, even for a man who has correctly enumerated the various partial goods.

It is necessary to tell the student that we have not fully answered his question. To do that would require a lengthy and elaborate analysis whereby we might be able to show him all the reasons for one precise ordering of goods as the only correct disposition of the parts of happiness. We shall have to be content with making two points about the order and proportion of partial goods. First, the order of these goods, like the enumeration of their variety, depends upon our understanding of the various capacities of human nature in their relation to one another. Second, it depends upon our recognition of what is distinctively human, in contrast to that part of his nature which man shares with brute animals. In the order of partial goods, those are higher which fulfill man's rational capacities; the lower goods are objects commonly pursued by men and animals. The lower serve the higher as means serve ends; in order to live *well*, we must first *live*. We struggle to subsist, not merely to be alive, but to live as *humanly* as possible, and this means subordinating and proportioning the goods which fulfill our animal capacities so that we shall be able to enjoy a fuller life than animals can lead—enriched by goods that fulfill capacities which only we, as men, possess. Just as a true conception of human nature is indispensable to a true conception of happiness, with respect to the variety of goods, so is it also with respect to their order. And the student is wrong in supposing that the point about the essential difference between men and brutes is dispensable. It is indispensable to a true conception of human happiness, and equally with respect to both aspects of its constitution—both the variety and the order of its parts.

I am sorry that you insist upon this last point, the student says, because it is a stumbling block in the way of my agreement with you. You simply haven't proved the point in any way, and, without obstinacy, I must stand on what I know—which is contrary to what you say is the case. I can see, however, that, assuming what you say to be true, the rest follows. And even though you have not given me the analysis which shows the precise order of the partial goods, I can surmise how that might be done. But I am still worried about the *possibility* of happiness, as you have defined it. I still don't see how it is possible for a man to be happy if he has to possess every sort of good thing altogether and at once.

The very language the student has used in raising this question is crucial to the answer. Strictly speaking, a man cannot ever *be* happy. He can only *become* happy. A human life is something in the process of becoming. It is a temporal whole, the parts of which cannot coexist. A life is a whole only in the way in which a day or a game is a whole—as an orderly succession of moments. The becoming of the whole is not completed until the process is acutally finished. That is why Solon, a wise man of ancient Greece, made what at first seems to be a paradoxical point, namely, that you cannot tell whether a man is happy until he is dead. Stated less paradoxically, the point is that happiness is the quality of a whole life, not of its parts. Another ancient, the Roman Boethius, defined happiness as the state of those made perfect by the possession in aggregate of all good things. The student may think that this is the definition of happiness we have been employing. His attention must be called, therefore, to two important differences. First, happiness may be the *state* of immortal souls in eternity—and that is probably what Boethius had in mind—but in this life, which is from beginning to end a process, a becoming, happiness is never realized *statically*. In the realm of time and change, it must exist *dynamically*—coming to be just as the life which it pervades becomes complete in time. Second, in so far as the happiness we have defined is a quality of this temporal life, the possession of all good things must be successive; it cannot be a simultaneous aggregate. Modifying the words of Boethius, we can define temporal happiness as a whole life made perfect by the successive enjoyment of all good things. Thus understood, there is nothing impossible about becoming happy, any more than it is impossible to complete a whole life by living from day to day.

It may be useful here to remind the student that a man cannot become happy by making *one* decision. A man becomes happy only through making many decisions, choosing many times between one particular good and another, exercising countless preferences. If a *single* decision could do it, the man who made it correctly could *be* happy as a result. But even a man who has correctly conceived happiness may fail to become happy unless the many choices he has to make from day to to day conform to the pattern of life he has conceived—a whole rounded out by every sort of good. Acts of choice or preference are always with respect to means, to partial goods. Throughout life we are forever at work putting the parts together to form the whole. The student should now be able to see how the problem of preference is solved in general, if not in detail. Faced with a choice between objects which are particular instances of partial goods, we *should* choose in such a way that we make progress toward the possession—in our life as a whole—of all good things. The end we have in view determines our choice of the means; our conception of the whole determines our manipulation of the parts.

It has been said that the means *are* the end in the process of becoming. This is the sum of moral knowledge. In the building of a life, as in the building of a house, it is true that as the parts are properly chosen and properly put together, the perfection of the whole gradually becomes. In every particular case, the ultimate criterion of choice is the end: the choice is right or wrong according as the realization of the end is furthered or hindered. At the beginning of life *all good things* is a possibility; when life is over, the possibility either has been realized or not, and that will depend upon the choices which have been made. The universal principles of moral knowledge consist of rules about the end to be sought and about the means to be chosen. If the end is properly conceived, the rules about the means will be properly formulated, since the conception of the end, when fully developed, consists of an ordering and proportioning of the means. If a man knows *what* he *should* seek, he will know *how* he *should* seek it. Based upon human nature, the rules of morality, directing us toward our end and prescribing our choice of means, have universality in the sense that they are the same for every man, but this does not mean that any man can avoid the task of applying these generalities according to the peculiar conditions of his individual life, and the particular circumstances of each case in which a choice must be made. And since these rules are the work of reason, not the gift of instinct, the moral judgments of men, about end or means, are susceptible to error.

I think I see, the student says, how what you have called a true conception of the end of life is a first principle from which all the rest can be derived. I know I don't see the detailed steps here, but that would be too much to expect. I do understand how, in a general way, the problem of preference is solved—at least in so far as the value to be placed on different things in relation to one another follows from what you have called the order and proportion of goods, which in turn follows from the way in which we conceive happiness to be constituted as a whole of parts. I am sure I don't understand any of this well enough to know how to think correctly in a particular case, facing particular alternatives—assuming, of course, that I had previously thought correctly about the end, and through it about the means in general. But what bothers me most of all is still the point about the violability of moral rules. Am I right in supposing, from what you have said, that men fail to do what they should do simply because of bad thinking— wrongly conceiving happiness, which means making errors about the order or variety of goods, and consequently misjudging the relative worth of objects in particular cases of preference?

No, the student must be told at once, to suppose that all misconduct —bad choices leading to bad acts—follows from bad thinking is itself a great error in thinking, as a matter of fact, a famous one in the history of moral theory. The quickest way to show the student that bad think- ing is *only one* of the sources of misconduct is to remind him of some- thing we saw toward the close of the first part of our discussion—when we still supposed pleasure to be the only criterion of preference. Re- member the rule of conduct we had then formulated: "In any case in which a choice can be made, men *should* prefer the alternative which, in the long run or viewing life as a whole, maximizes pleasure and mini- mizes displeasure." The student should now be able to see how that rule contains in germ almost all the truth we have subsequently dis- covered, for the maxim could be thus rephrased: in any case in which a choice can be made, men *should* prefer the alternative which, consider- ing the possibility of living a whole life well, tends to realize the possi- bility of happiness. Now we saw, in our earlier discussion, that the rule is violable in two ways. We distinguished between two sorts of mistakes we can make—mistakes of calculation and mistakes of acting contrary to our calculations. Even though a man has thought correctly about the end and the means in general, and in this sense knows what is really good for him, he may in a particular case be seduced by what is apparently better at that time, even though it is *really worse* in the long run.

Men are not simply *rational* beings. They are rational *animals*. They are creatures of passion, of animal appetites, but they are also capable of abstract thought, by which they can form a conception of happiness and of the goods in general which constitute it. All the goods we have been talking about—happiness itself, or the various *kinds* of partial goods—are rational or intelligible objects. They certainly cannot be perceived by the senses, although particular instances of the partial goods may somehow present themselves in that way. But precisely because man is a creature of sense as well as of reason, and because his desires can be determined by what he senses as well as by his abstract thinking, the alternatives which he faces in particular cases of preference are, as objects, both sensible and intelligible, and make their appeal both to his animal appetite and to his will—the latter being the desire for objects rationally judged to be good, the former being the desire for what is sensed as good.

We cannot here fully explain all the psychological points that are involved. For our present purposes, suffice it to say that, in the conflict between sensible and intelligible goods, the former may win out because they are *apparently* better at the time, though not *really* better in terms of the conception of life as a whole. Whenever they do win out, you have a case in which misconduct is due to weakness of will, rather than error in thought. Instead of following the dictates of reason, a man may choose according to the promptings of his passions. Thus we see that the violation of moral truth has two sources: one, bad thinking—misconception of the end, and of the means in general; the other, weak willing—preference for the *apparent* good, under the influence of the passions, rather than for the real good which reason has determined. And we also see how the very nature of human morality (revealed to us by the sources of misconduct) depends on the nature of man—his essential distinction from brute animals. For, lacking reason, animals know and desire only through sense and instinct; lacking reason, they are not able to conceive their end, and hence cannot misconceive it; lacking reason, their desires are all instinctively determined and subject to whatever objects dominate the sensible present, whereas men have free will to choose between sensible and intelligible goods. In short, unlike animals, men can be moral or immoral according as they think well or poorly, and according as, in the exercise of their free will, they act according to what right reason prescribes, or contrary to it.

There is no point in going any further, the student finally says. I told you before that I wasn't prepared to accept your assumption about an essential difference between men and animals. I am even more opposed to it now that I see it includes the notion of free will. You were quite fair to admit that you had not, and probably could not here, explain all the psychological points that are involved; but until you do explain them, until you do prove that human thinking is different from animal intelligence, and above all until you can show what you mean by free will and that there is such a thing, it would be unprofitable to carry our discussion any further. I am willing to agree that your conclusions have cogency for anyone who grants your hypotheses. *If* man is peculiarly rational, *if* man has this mysterious free will, *then* you are right about morality, and its principles, and the way they can be violated. Until I agree to these *ifs,* my position is exactly what it was when we started—though perhaps, I should admit that I now understand better the theory which I, as a moral skeptic, have been rejecting. In fact, I can now give you more clearly the basic reason for my moral skepticism. It is simply that men do not have free will. If I had not let you somehow obfuscate this point at the beginning, our discussion would have stopped almost as soon as it started. I tried to tell you at the very start that I didn't think there was any problem of preference; I tried to say there was no *why* for any choice, no *why* in the sense of a reason which justified it, but only a cause. Every choice a man *appears* to make is just like any *choice* an animal makes. It is no choice at all, but a pre-determined event—arising from instinctive determinations, and all the accidental conditionings which have occurred in the course of life up to that point. If there is no problem of preference, because there is no free will, then all the rest of our discussion was totally beside the point. Or, to put it another way, there is a problem of preference, but only for the psychologist who tries to find the *causes* of behavior and to *describe* what men and animals in fact do; but there is no problem for the moralist who tries to find the *reasons* for human conduct and to *prescribe* what men should do. If I am right about the facts, then you must admit that the moral skeptic is justified in thinking that all the different moral systems which men have invented— yours among them—are nothing but intricate and elaborate rationalizations, fostered by the delusion that men are free.

The student is right that there is no point in going further without

first satisfying him on the major psychological questions which under-
lie all moral discourse. It would not be sufficient here to remind him
that he did admit certain *facts,* such as that men do appear to act contrary to their best lights and seem to suffer repentance for their folly—
facts which *suggest* human freedom. He rightly asks for proof, and
the task of proof in this case is long and arduous, as it is also on the
other point about man's rationality as his essential ditinction from
brutes.   All of this requires another and separate discussion, one in
which we would probably find the student a skeptic about the truths of
philosophical psychology. We might then discover that his moral skepticism was rooted in a deeper doubt—the doubt about the validity of
any philosophical knowledge.

By way of concluding this discussion, it might, however, be worth
while to remind him of one thing. He has learned one truth which he
may not have known before. All through the discussion he has admitted seeing the connection between human nature and the principles
of human morality. Now if our hypotheses concerning human nature
and human freedom can be affirmed, then he must admit the consequences (and he has indicated his willingness to do so), namely, the
conception of happiness, the order and variety of goods, and the principles by which the moral problem of preference can be solved. Furthermore, since whatever human nature is it is the same for men at all times
and everywhere, the student must also agree that there cannot be a
number of different "moral systems" each equally acceptable. He must
agree that there is only one true doctrine, only one which accords with
the truth about human nature, just as he agreed that in the light of
human nature there is only one right interpretation of the natural moral
law to seek *the* good, only one right conception of happiness and of
the means thereto.

If the student wonders where this discussion would turn next— were
it continued after the psychological questions had been satisfactorily
answered—we should, in parting, tell him that what remains to be considered is the very heart of moral knowledge, namely, *good* habits (which
the ancients denominated virtues), and especially the habits of right desire and right action which are called the moral virtues. All the princi-

ples we have so far discussed become operative only through virtue. The virtues must be possessed, not only as among the goods which are constitutive means of happiness, but also as a special sort of means—generative of happiness. And this is especially true of the moral virtues, which are habits of right choice in particular cases, habits which have been formed in the light of a proper ordering of goods and which enable us to act according to reason, to prefer the real to the apparent good. The major part of moral theory, therefore, is concerned with the definition of these virtues, and with the rules for acquiring them.

We have previously said that the means *are* the end in the process of becoming. The end is rightly understood only so far as we rightly apprehend the means which constitute it. It is also true that the end is possessed at any moment only to the extent that we possess the means which generate it—the habits from which our conduct flows. At any given moment in his life a man is more or less on the way to becoming happy according to the state of his habits, especially the *moral* habits— the virtues or vices—which make his *character* what it is. Aristotle thus summarized the whole of his *Ethics* when he said. "According as a man's character is, so does the end appear to him." Until a life is over, you cannot judge whether it *is* a happy one; but so far as you can see into a man's character, you can tell, even while life is going on, whether a man is *becoming* happy.

CHAPTER V.

PSYCHOLOGICAL PRESUPPOSITIONS: LIMITATIONS OF THE DIALECTIC.

IN THE preceding chapters of this book, I have outlined a dialectical procedure whereby a doubting mind might be led to the recognition of moral truth. What has been given is the bare plot of a conversation between teacher and student. The student was, at the beginning, a skeptic about moral matters, denying the objectivity of moral knowledge, supposing that all moral judgments were a matter of opinion, entirely relative to the individual or to his cultural location at a given time and place. The teacher, by asking him to explain the undeniable fact that men exercise preference, gradually made him realize that his own criteria for preference — pleasure and quantity of pleasure — had a certain universal validity; and then, as a result of seeing the inadequacy of these criteria, the student began to understand that happiness, rather than pleasure, was the ultimate principle of moral judgments. The crucial steps in the argument were: (1) the distinction between pleasure as one among many objects of desire and pleasure as the satisfaction of any desire; (2) the enumeration of the variety of goods which are objects of human desire; (3) the point that only the totality of goods can completely satisfy desire; (4) the realization that this totality of goods, leaving nothing to be desired, is the end of all our seeking, and that everything else is sought for the sake of its attainment; (5) the conception of happiness as "all good things," a whole constituted by every type of good, the complete good being the end, the incomplete good its parts or constitutive means; (6) the conclusion that the end, as the first principle in the practical order, is the ultimate criterion of preference, for prefer- or choice is exercised only with respect to means, and hence we should, in every case, prefer whatever is more conducive to the attainment of happiness.

But, unfortunately, this dialectical process was far from being completed. The student may have gained some understanding of the position he had previously rejected. He was not, however, convinced that happiness, rightly conceived, is the same for all men — the same order and variety of goods. Nor did he admit that rules of conduct, even if they are universal, can be violated by a disobedience born of man's freedom to act for or against his own real good. Conviction on these major points could be produced, the student indicated, only if he could be shown the truth of certain views about human nature, which the teacher seemed to be taking for granted. And the teacher, on his side, had to acknowledge that unless men were rational animals, unless in being rational they were essentially distinct from brutes, specifically superior in their powers, and through their rationality possessing freedom of will, unless these things were so, the proof of moral principles could not be made. Indeed, the very "fact" of preference, with which the whole discussion had started, turned out to be ambiguous, since the teacher, assuming free will, had supposed preference to be a genuine choice among alternatives, and the student, denying freedom, had regarded preference as if it were a mechanically determined motion.

That the argument thus uncovered its own limitations is one of the chief merits of the dialectical procedure. The student learned an hypothetical line of reasoning; more than that, he acknowledged its cogency: the premises, being granted, the conclusion seemed to follow. But the premises were certainly not self-evident truths; and, since it is not fitting in philosophy to make assumptions or regard conclusions as merely hypothetical, the psychological propositions upon which the whole argument turned must themselves be demonstrated. A dialectic of morals cannot be made conclusive unless prior matters are *similarly* argued. I say *"similarly* argued" because it is not enough to see that metaphysics and psychology provide the theoretical foundations for moral philosophy; it must also be recognized that the psychological questions involved are for the philosopher, not for the scientist, to answer, and that his mode of answering these questions must be dialectical *in the sense that dialectic is the process of inductive reasoning whereby the mind establishes those primary truths which are not self-*

evident.[12] The proposition that man is a rational animal is not self-evident. Its truth can be established only after it has been inductively proved that a plurality of individual substances exists and that among these corporeal substances there are differences in essence as well as in number. For if there are no substances and if they do not differ essentially, as well as accidentally, from one another, there is no point in attempting to define man's specific nature. That man exists as a distinct species of corporeal substance is the ultimate conclusion of a dialectic which is many times more difficult and much more elaborate in its phases than the dialectic of morals herein described. Without undertaking it, the teacher cannot convince the student of even the simplest moral truths — that preference involves free choice or that happiness, being the same ultimate end for all men, is the universal principle

---

12. Two meanings of "induction" as well as two meanings of "dialectic" must be distinguished. The word "induction" is sometimes used to name the non-discursive step by which the mind generalizes from experience: just as it abstracts universal concepts from sensible particulars, so it sometimes forms, in the light of these concepts themselves and without the mediation of prior knowledge, universally true judgments. Because they are not obtained by reasoning, these judgments are called propositions *per se nota* or self-evident truths; and the intellectual act by which they are achieved can be called an "intuitive induction." (Vd. Aristotle, *Post. Anal.*, II, 19). In contrast to intuitive induction, there is that process of the mind which might be called "rational induction," because it involves reasoning, and is a discursive or mediated way of knowing, a process and not a single step. Such reasoning or proof is inductive rather than deductive in that it is *a posteriori* rather than *a priori*, from effects to causes rather than from causes to effects. In contrast to deductive reasoning, which explicitly elaborates what is contained in universal truths already known, inductive reasoning establishes those primary truths which are affirmations of existence, truths which are neither self-evident nor capable of being deduced from prior universals. The ultimate grounds of inductive proof are the facts of sense-experience. The *a posteriori* proof of the *existence* of God is *inductive* reasoning in this precise sense. Whereas deductive reasoning is the motion of the mind from what is more knowable in itself to what is less knowable in itself, inductive reasoning is that motion in which the mind goes from what is more knowable to us to the existence of something whose nature is more knowable in itself, though less knowable to us.

The word "dialectic" is frequently used, in the Aristotelian tradition, to name probable reasoning from premises taken for granted for the sake of argument. But that is not the only traditional meaning of the word. There is, of course, the Platonic meaning of dialectic as the motion of the mind toward first principles, but there is also the Aristotelian point that "dialectic is a process of criticism wherein lies the path to the principles of all enquiries" (*Topics*, I, 1). When dialectic is employed demonstratively and not polemically, it is identical with inductive reasoning directed, not to all first principles or the principles of all enquiries (for some of these are self-evident and are known by intuitive induction), but only to those primary affirmations of existence which are neither self-evident nor capable of deductive demonstration. As reasoning may be either deductive or inductive, so demonstration may be either "scientific" (i.e., deductive) or "dialectical" (i.e., inductive).

which directs men in their choice of means.[13]

Since the student is justified in not considering the argument to be conclusive until his basic objections have been met (i.e., until his questions about prior matters have been answered), I am willing to regard whatever conclusions we have so far reached as *hypothetical,* for that is the only way in which the student can now understand them. I do so in order to go on, not with the dialectic itself, but with a deductive elaboration of some of its major points. In the final section of this essay, I shall try to show how the two fundamental concepts of ethics — happiness and virtue — are indispensable to political philosophy; for unless these concepts have objective validity, unless there is an objective order of goods, an order of means and ends, which enables us to distinguish right from wrong in human conduct, by knowledge rather than by opinion, the philosopher has no defense against *realpolitik* (which is an inevitable consequence of positivism in the sphere of politics.) And in

---

13. The argument which must be undertaken can be called "a dialectic of substance, essence, and man." I think I am now able to work out the several phases of this argument, and, having outlined the whole of it as an orderly sequence of parts, I am satisfied that it demonstrates, with certitude, a number of primary propositions which have heretofore always been assumed—not because anyone could have mistaken them as self-evident, but because the way of inductive reasoning and dialectical demonstration has been inadequately understood and too infrequently used in philosophy. I hope to be able to publish this material shortly, and with it I shall try to present a more analytically refined account of inductive and deductive reasoning than can be given in a brief footnote. Vd. fn. 12, *supra.* The "dialectic of substance, essence, and man" is not only important in itself as an argument for certain conclusions which have not previously been demonstrated; but it is also significant as an illustration of hitherto unnoted aspects of philosophical method.

In one sense, the argument is miscalled a dialectic, for all of its phases are not strictly inductive, though the denomination is justified by the fact that all of the primary conclusions are inductively reached. Thus, for example, the proof that, *if* there are a number of distinct essences, they *must* be ordered in a perfect hierarchy, is deductive. (This proof, by the way, was given only in the indirect form of a *reductio ad absurdum* argument in *The Solution of the Problem of Species,* The Thomist, III, 2, pp. 329-332. In that form, the proposition that man is a rational animal and superior to all other corporeal creatures, had to be assumed. But the definition of man, not being self-evident, must itself be proved, and that cannot be accomplished, unless the perfect hierarchy of essences can itself be independently proved. Hence, the importance of a direct proof.) But that there are a number of distinct essences embodied in the world of corporeal substances, how many there are, and what they are, must be proved inductively from the observable motions and operations of sensible things, and this can be done only if we first know that perceived objects, which *seem* to be subjects of change, are truly substances composed of matter and forms, and that among these forms one must be substantial and all the rest accidental. From these facts, inductively proved, the truth about the hierarchy of essences can be deduced; and from the truth about hierarchy can be developed the criteria for interpreting the sensible evidences from which we must induce the existence of whatever essential distinctions there are among substances.

the subsequent section of this essay, I propose to treat of three matters insufficiently discussed in the foregoing dialectic: (1) the objectivity of the good in relation to desire; (2) the kinds of good and the types of means-end relationships; and (3) the nature of virtue as principal means to happiness as end. All of these points were implicated in the preceding discussions, and would have been explicated had the discussions continued. In each case, I shall indicate a leading quistion the student might have asked at a given turn in the preceding discussions — a question which, if fully explored, would have then generated another separate phase of inquiry. But now, for the sake of brevity, I shall confine myself to an analytic summary, outlining in each case what any teacher would have to do to carry on.[14]

---

14. It should be recognized that brevity is the real reason for this change in style. Although the full development of argument with respect to each of the three points mentioned, would depend upon psychological propositions already questioned by the student, there is no reason why the student should not proceed *hypothetically*—to discover whether other moral truths (other than the one about happiness) can be established, once it is granted that man is a rational animal, that man has a nature and powers essentially distinct from the nature and powers of brute animals, that man has free will, etc. If the student had been told, at the very beginning of the discussion, that these psychological propositions were indispensable to the argument, he would either have refused to begin until these propositions had been proved, or have rightly insisted that any conclusions reached by an argument thus undertaken must be regarded as hypothetical. That is the way he now views the conclusion about happiness (as constituted in the same way for all men). There is no reason, therefore, why he would be unwilling similarly to entertain further conclusions about the order of goods or about virtue, if they could be reached. But to deal argumentatively with each of the three points, now to be considered, would require much more time and patience than can be expected of the reader. That is why I shall present an analytical summary of the argument instead of letting it expand in response to the demands of an inquiring mind.

On the dependence of ethics and politics upon psychology, see Aristotle's *Ethics*, I, 13.

CHAPTER VI.

REAL VS. APPARENT GOODS: THE REALITY
OF VIRTUE.

1. THE GOOD AS OBJECT OF DESIRE

WHEN THE word "good" was first introduced to name "any
object of desire,"[15] the student might have stopped the discussion, or turned it into other channels, by asking whether this was
not a mere tautology, a mere rule of verbal substitution (i.e., the
word "good" being substitutable for "object of desire" and conversely). For such a question would have raised a crucial issue concerning
the relation of these two basic terms: *either* whatever is called "good"
is so called *because* it is in fact desired by someone; *or* whatever
anyone desires is desired *because* it is good. In the first alternative,
there could be no distinction between the real and the apparent good,
since the fact of desire itself is regarded as conferring goodness upon
its object. In the second alternative, goodness would be a property
of things apart from their being actually desired, for as good they
would be *desirable* whether or not *desired,* in which case no object
would be really good unless it were desirable according to its being,
whereas any object whose goodness derived simply from its being desired might be an *apparent* good. It is plain that the alternative which
destroys the distinction between real and apparent goods results in complete subjectivism (and the denial of moral knowledge). Only the alternative which maintains this distinction can uphold the objectivity of
good. Only if it is possible to desire things because they are good (and,
as such, desired), can desires themselves be objectively judged as right
or wrong (i.e., according to the goodness or badness of their objects).[16]

---

15. Vd. Chapter III, *supra*, p. 39.

16. This issue was briefly considered at one point in the dialectic. Vd. Chapter III,
supra, pp. 43-44: If "the objects we have called goods are good only because they

Such traditional maxims as that "the good is what all desire" or that "goodness is being in relation to appetite or desire," do not solve the problem. On the contrary, they raise the problem by calling for an interpretation which will show how goodness is founded in being prior to actual desire (i.e., to human desires determined by judgments or estimations of objects as good or bad.)[17] The problem cannot be solved, nor can the familiar maxims about goodness, being, and desire, be rightly interpreted, unless we distinguish between "natural desire" and "human (or animal) desire" and until we understand that the good is being as a final cause of motion. Then it will be seen that whatever is imperfect, through privation of being in some determinate respect, has determined potentialities for perfection; each determinate potentiality is a natural appetite or desire for some actualizing determination of the thing's nature; any thing's natural appetite or desire is constituted by all its determinate potencies, whether these be powers which flow from its essence or mere potentialities determined by privation through the thing's possession of contrary forms; each potency has

---

are desired"; if "there is always a relativity of the good to actual desire," then "we shall never be able to say what men *should* desire, which is central to moral knowledge as normative or prescriptive. In order to get beyond a mere description of what men *do* desire, we must somehow show the student that the objects men desire, they desire *because they judge them to be good*." But in the discussion itself, this problem was inadequately solved by proposing an ultimate end, which in fact all men do desire, namely, to live well; and in terms of this end, we argued that men *should* desire whatever is necessary for the attainment of this end. This is a partial solution, since it is true that the goodness of means may be derived from the goodness of the end they serve; but it leaves two major questions unanswered: (1) is the end good simply because all men do desire it, or because it is the ultimate good which all men should desire? and (2) are any of the means good in their own right, and apart from being means to the end, so that they, too, should be desired because they are intrinsically good (i.e., desirable)? The student permitted the discussion to go on at this point, although he could have stopped it by insisting upon a deeper examination into the meaning of the good as an object of desire.

17. Vd. St. Thomas Aquinas, *Summa Theologica*, I, qq. 5, 6. wherein these traditional maxims are not merely repeated but interpreted in such a way as to indicate the solution of the problem. It should be noted that in Q. 5, A. 1, St. Thomas says: "the essence of goodness consists in this, that it is in some way *desirable*" (Italics mine). Just as intelligibility is an aspect of being prior to its being actually understood, so desirability is an aspect of being prior to its being actually desired (i.e., by an elicit appetite).

a tendency (and appetite consists in such tendency) toward actual being; now that which actualizes a potency satisfies a natural desire or
tendency; to be actual in a certain respect is, therefore, the object of
every natural desire and this actuality is the final cause of the thing's
motion; hence, the good is being as *naturally desirable;* it is whatever
completes or perfects the being of a thing in respects in which it is imperfect or incomplete, the very respects which determine its potencies,
and hence its natural desires, for perfection. When "desire" is understood to signify *natural desire* and when "good' 'is understood to signify *actual being in relation to potency,* then it becomes intelligibly
true to say that "the good is what all desire" or that "goodness is being in relation to appetite." In fact, these become self-evident truths,
which must be affirmed as soon as their terms are thus understood. It is
similarly true that each thing *has* as much goodness as it *has* being (i.e.,
actuality); and it might also be added that each thing has as much desire for goodness as it is deprived of the being that is due its nature, i.e.,
relative to its capacities for perfection. In these meanings of "good"
and of "desire," there is a strict correlation between them, for potency,
as material cause, is at every point correlative with actuality, as final
cause. Hence it is possible to say without contradiction that the object
of desire is good *because* it is desired and also that whatever is desired
is desirable *because* it is good, although the priority of actuality and of
final causes gives the second statement a certain precedence over the
first.[18]

---

18. St. Thomas makes a fourfold distinction: between being simply and being
relatively, good relatively and good simply. A thing is a being simply according to its
first actuality or essence; a thing has being relatively according to its second acts, or
those accidental determinations which accrue to it from its own operations or its being
acted upon. But a thing is said to be good relatively with respect to the actuality of its
nature (i.e., its essence and powers), whereas it has goodness or perfection simply
according as its nature is completed in being by second acts. Vd. *Summa Theologica,*
I, 5, 1, ad 1. In the light of these distinctions, the goods which are the objects of
natural desire are the actualities which constitute the relative being of a thing; the good
relatively is never an object of desire, unless it be on the part of prime matter, which is
the potency for being simply.

The interpretation of natural desire and of being as good in relation thereto must
be differently made for non-living and living substances, since the former, in all their
accidental motions, pass from contrary to contrary, and hence never increase in perfection of being; whereas the latter, having impassible powers and being capable of
immanent activity, can acquire perfections without privation of contrary forms, and can,
therefore, grow in perfection of being. This is especially true of man whose specifically
human powers are capable of habituation.

But this account of the good as an object of desire is purely metaphysical: in terms of potency conceived as appetitive or tendential, and of actuality conceived as perfecting or good. This account of desire and the desirable as correlative aspects of being in motion would be true even if there were no human beings, even if there were no creatures who felt pleasure and pain, who consciously yearned for objects they deemed desirable, or who experienced satisfaction or frustration.[19] We must, therefore, not confuse the metaphysical conception of the good with the moralist's conception, which concerns the good of man, or the variety of goods for man. As metaphysically considered, the good is not subject to the distinction between real and apparent; but in the moralist's consideration, this is obviously an indispensable distinction. Our task is to discover how this distinction can be made in the realm of the human good, with which the moralist is concerned. The problem can be solved only if we see the human good in relation to the natural good, and this in turn depends upon the basic distinction between human and natural desire. Human desire is *conscious* desire. The word "conscious" is here used in its primary signification: it means "with or through knowledge." A human desire is an appetite determined to its object by knowledge of this object — not merely theoretical knowledge, but practical knowledge consisting in a judgment that the object is good. The appetite which is thus determined is not *any* potency; it is a specific power of man, the very nature of which is to tend toward an object intellectually apprehended as good. Human desire can be defined, therefore, as the *act* of man's intellectual appetite, i.e., his special

---

19. This account would be untrue only if there were no world of creatures at all—no imperfect beings, subject to natural desire because of their imperfect natures. Furthermore, the actual separation between desire and the good which quiets it, can occur only in a world of temporal beings, beings in motion, for where change is not possible, there either desire must be forever unrequited or desire does not exist at all because the good is possessed. This indicates that our metaphysical understanding of the good as being in relation to desire is primarily in terms of being in motion—the realm of corporeal and temporal creatures. Goodness in the domain of spiritual and aeviternal creatures, and the goodness of God, are dimly intelligible to us only by remotion and analogy. The Divine goodness is as infinitely unlike the goodness of changing things as the pure actuality of Divine being differs from the actuality of beings composite of potency and act.

power of desiring or tending toward what his intellect apprehends as good. The distinction between human and natural desire is thus seen to be twofold: in the first place, a human desire is always an *act* (of a power,) and never identical with mere potency or power itself, whereas every discriminable natural desire is identical with some potency or power, having by its very nature a determinate tendency; and, in the second place, natural desire is unconscious, i.e., it is totally independent of knowledge of the object desired, whereas human desire must always be conscious, for it is the act of a power which cannot be moved to act except by a prior act of apprehension.[20]

In the light of the foregoing, we can define the *natural* good as the naturally *desirable,* as comprising the objects of all natural desire; and the *human* good as the consciously *desired,* as comprising all the objects of human desire, of both intellectual and sensitive appetite. Now a third term must be introduced, namely, the *natural human* good, for man has, over and above his two conscious appetites, as many natural desires as he has powers and potencies which follow determinately from the essence and accidents of his nature. The natural human good comprises all those objects toward which human nature tends as toward per-

---

20. It is important to mention, but not necessary to develop here, the distinction between the two conscious appetites which man possesses: the sensitive appetite, the power of tending toward sensible objects which the sensitive powers estimate to be good or pleasant; and the intellectual appetite, already defined. Only the latter is specifically human (i.e., possessed by man alone), whereas the former the brutes also possess. Animal desires (acts of the sensitive appetite) are distinguished from natural desires by the same two criteria which distinguish human desire. It should be noted that the sensitive appetite is not moved by a mere apprehension of the sensible object, but, as in the case of intellectual appetite, only by an estimation of the object apprehended as good or bad, pleasant or unpleasant—whether this estimation be the work of instinct (conditioned or unmodified) as in the case of brutes, or the work of the cogitative power in the case of man, i.e., that power of interior sensitivity which is usually called "the particular reason," because it operates with the help of reason in judging sensible things as fitting or harmful. The distinction between intellectual and sensitive appetite is important, not only because of its bearing on the imperfect voluntariness of brute behavior in contrast to the perfect voluntariness and freedom of specifically human acts; but also because the conflict of these two appetites in man explains how man can act contrary to true rational judgments concerning what *should* be done or sought. In the latter connection, the distinction bears on the problem of the real vs. the apparent good.

fections of its being in respects in which it is deprived of actuality.[21] The whole problem turns on the discrepancy between the human good and the natural human good. The natural human good is a specific case of the good that the metaphysician defines as the act of being which can terminate a natural desire: it is merely the good or the desirable appropriate to the nature of man. But the object of human desire may or may not be naturally good, by the metaphysical criterion. Men can be mistaken both in their rational judgments and their sensitive estimations: they can consider things to be good, which, when consciously desired and subsequently possessed, ultimately frustrate their natural desires. They can, in short, consciously desire objects which they do not want or want for things they fail to desire because of deficiencies in apprehension or errors in judgment; and even when their desires somehow conform to their wants, the way in which they order the objects they consciously desire may prevent them from achieving the fulfillment of their natural appetites. That which is an object of actual human desire (i.e., of an act of intellectual or sensitive appetite) may not be the *real* good, in the metaphysical sense of that which, in the order of real being, perfects the nature of man. Whereas the object of natural desire, in the case of human or any other nature, is necessarily a real good, the object of conscious human desire may be an *apparent* good, strictly not a good at all, but evil either because unsuitable to nature or as relative to other objects of desire. The apparent good is, therefore, good only *because* it is actually desired, which means, of course, that the object is good only in human judgment or estimation, upon which the desire itself is consequent. The real good is, in contrast, always an object desirable in itself, as a perfection of the nature:

---

21. Natural human desires are, of course, natural in precisely the same sense as the natural desires of the stone or of the plant. They are unconscious: the objects of natural human desire are not, as such, apprehended, judged or estimated. And natural human desires are determinate as potencies or powers, not as acts. This may help to explain what we mean when, in the case of man, we speak of his "unconscious desires." Such desires are not the acts of his consciously determinable appetitive powers. They are rather identical with the striving or tendency of his powers themselves—all the powers, vegetative, as well as sensitive and rational, and in the latter case, apprehensive as well as appetitive. It might be clarifying to use the word "wants" to name the natural appetites of man, in contrast to the word "desires" to name his conscious appetitive acts. This would enable us to deal with obvious phenomena of human behaviour—cases in which men are impelled by wants without knowing what they seek because the want has not yet been elevated to the level of desire by knowledge of the appetible object.

hence when it becomes, through knowledge and right judgment, the object of actual human desire, it is desired *because* it is good. Whatever men actually desire, they apprehend under the aspect of the good, for in order to desire any object they must judge it to be good, whether they do it rightly or wrongly. And what ultimately determines whether their judgment is right or wrong — whether the object actually desired is a real or an apparent good — is human nature itself, its natural appetites and the natural goods toward which they tend. In proportion as his moral judgments are founded on a correct and adequate understanding of his nature, will a man make a true estimation of what is really good.[22]

This understanding of the good as object of desire has two further consequences, beyond enabling us to distinguish the real from the apparent good. Both must be considered before we pass to a discussion of the order and variety of goods.

In the first place, we can define the precise metaphysical character of every object of desire, natural or conscious. By the essence of what the good is in relation to desire, the object of desire must always be a change or motion, for change or motion is *the act of that which is in potentiality in a respect in which it is potential.* Since the good is always the act of being toward which potencies or powers tend, and by which such tendencies are terminated, the object of desire must be a change or motion, i.e., an actualization. The full significance of this is seen by comparing the object of knowledge with the object of desire:

---

22. It does not follow that a man who, judging aright, desires what is really good, will necessarily act accordingly; for in the conflict between his sensitive and his rational appetites, an apparent good may dominate his conduct at the moment of action. Vd. Aristotle's account of incontinence in the *Ethics*, Bk. VII, 3. All that is here being said is that the basic truths which constitute ethical *theory*—truths about the variety and order of objects which are really good for man—rest on metaphysical and psychological knowledge, the former concerning the foundation of goodness in being, the latter concerning the foundation of the real human good in the nature of man. The real human good is the natural human good as apprehended and thus become an object of conscious desire; the human good, taken without qualification, is not identical with the natural human good, for it includes all the apparent goods which are the objects of mistaken judgments. If the word "good" be restricted in its signification to mean "real good," then the metaphysical statement that the good is what all desire is true only for the objects of natural desire, human or otherwise; it certainly is not true for the objects of conscious human desire, since what all men desire, consciously, may be either really or apparently good.

the object of knowledge is always the completed nature of some existing thing (i.e., a substance, in its essential or accidental determinations),
and furthermore, the object of knowledge is primarily the nature of another, and only secondarily, in reflexive knowledge, the nature of the
knower; in contrast, the objects of desire are always perfections with
respect to which a nature is incomplete, and furthermore, the objects
of desire are primarily perfections to be accomplished by changes in
one's self, and only secondarily by changes in other things.[23] In short,
the objects of desire are always future acts. The acts, or the motions
which they terminate, must be future, for were they present or accomplished, potency or desire would be abolished. This definition of desire's object holds, in the case of conscious human desires, for the apparent as well as for the real good. The object which is apprehended as
good to have — whether by sense or intellect, whether truly or falsely
— is never a substance or any determinate aspect of its completed
nature (because such an object could not possibly be desired, and nothing except the desirable can be apprehended as good), but always a
change in a substance, in some respect in which it is deprived of actual
being.

This truth is frequently overlooked or obscured because we speak
loosely of objects of desire as if they were *existing things:* we name
objects of desire by using the same words we use to name objects of
our theoretic knowledge. Not only does this falsify the contingency of
objects of desire as future acts, but it also obscures the fact that the
primary objects of desire are changes in one's self, and not in another.

---

23. This distinction between the object of desire and the object of knowledge
accounts for the radical difference between theoretic and practical truth: only when
the object is an already determinate nature can truth be in the intellect by conformity
to what is; since the object of desire is also the object of our practical judgments, and
since this object is always a future contingent event, i.e., a change to be accomplished,
the truth of practical judgments cannot be by conformity to what is, but must be by
conformity of the judgment to right desire, i.e., desire for a real good, an object of
natural desire.

Furthermore, it should be noted that the true *is* not an object; rather, being an act
of knowledge, it, like the act of desire, *has* an object. The good, on the other hand, is
an object both of (practical) knowledge and of desire. The good is not only an object,
but an act of being. The radical difference between the true and the good is that the
true is an act in the order of intentional existence, whereas the good is an act in the
order of real existence.

When we talk about desiring this thing or that — as if the primary objects of desire were (like the primary objects of knowledge) things in the world about us — we tend to forget the profound metaphysical truth that everything desires its own perfection. For any substance to desire (naturally, of course) its own perfection, the objects it desires must be those still future changes or acts by which its being can be perfected. Furthermore, a substance cannot naturally desire anything except its own perfection: the good which is relative to the potency of some other substance can never be the object of natural desire on the part of this substance. But, as we know, the motions of other substances may be efficient or material causes of the actualization of this substance's potencies. Hence, the objects of natural desire may include, *secondarily*, changes in other things, in so far as these are causally involved. The good *of* anything consists in the perfections which are attainable by it: these are the primary objects of natural desire. The good *for* anything depends on the already possessed perfections of other things through which they can operate as efficient or material causes in the changes by which the thing itself attains perfection: these are the secondary objects of natural desire. In both cases, the object of desire is a change; in both cases, the good is a cause; but when the change is in the thing itself, the good is a final cause, whereas when the change is in some other thing, the good is an efficient or material cause.

If we apply these metaphysical insights to the human case, we see that man, like everything else in the world, naturally desires his own perfection; and since the real good is the object judged in conformity to natural desire, a man must desire his own perfection if he rightly conceive his good. Considering for the moment only real goods, the objects of conscious human desire divide into the goods *of* man and the goods *for* man: the former consisting in those changes in himself by which a man achieves greater perfection, more complete actuality; the latter consisting in those changes in other things which cooperate, materially or efficiently, in the change of man himself. Thus, a man's own acts and habits, and even perhaps his health, are goods *of* his nature, perfections which terminate his potencies; whereas, foodstuffs and clothing materials, all of the resources of physical nature which man can use for his own well-being, are goods *for* him. When we speak of all these other things as good for us, we are using the word "good" attributively, for we are not referring to the good which these things can attain, but the perfection they now possess, without which they could not assist us in changing ourselves.[24]

In the second place, we can now understand the distinction between happiness, as *the* good *of* man, and all the other goods which constitute it, whether these be, in themselves, goods of or for man. The natural desire of any thing can be regarded in two ways: either in terms of the substance as a unified whole of potencies and powers, or in terms of each of these potencies or powers, considered by itself. Viewed in the latter way, a thing has as many distinct natural desires as it has determinate potencies and powers; and accordingly there is a plurality of distinct objects which are the real goods of and for that thing. But every substance is a one, and its nature is a one, and so its powers and potencies (determined as they are by what it actually is) are not a mere aggregation but form a unity of ordered parts. Viewed in its unity, rather than as diversified, the natural desire of a substance must be for the good of the substance as a whole — the perfection, not of any single power or potency, but of them all. When it is said that each thing seeks its own perfection, this can be understood of each power or potency as a natural tendency toward its own actualization; but it can also, and must, be primarily understood of the substance itself, as a unity of diverse powers and potencies. Though the object peculiar to

---

24. I shall return to this distinction between goods of man and goods for man in a later discussion of means and ends. This distinction, made in terms of the axiom that everything seeks its own perfection, raises profound ethical problems which cannot be discussed here: for example, the whole problem of altruism and selfishness. Is man ever obligated to work for the good of any other thing, inanimate or animate, animal or human; and if so, how is this a real good, i.e., an object of natural desire, if it is not a good *for* man as well as a good *of* the other thing? This problem becomes particularly acute with respect to the relation of men in economic and political associations. In theology, this distinction is exemplified by the consideration of the Divine being and goodness as the ultimate good *for* man, whereas the vision of God is the ultimate good *of* man's soul. The theological case indicates, furthermore, that what is good for man may be superior to him in being, and its efficient causality in bringing about human perfection may be without human aid, except in the order of dispositive causality; whereas the material things which are good for man are not only inferior in being, but usually, if not always, require efficient causality on the part of man (the work of his art) to render them useful.

each power or potency, as a distinct natural desire, is a good *of* the substance, it is not the good of the substance as a whole, but only in part. The good of the substance as a whole must, therefore, be a complex object — not a simple one, but a one constituted as an ordered many. Viewing the substance as a whole, we see that its natural desire for its own perfection is the desire for this complex object — the unified realization of the multiple perfections terminating its various tendencies. Since a many can become one only through order, which reduces conflict and maximizes cooperation, the perfection of a substance as a whole must be an ordered whole of goods, in which the object of every distinct natural desire is represented, and each is achieved without loss or undue displacement of the others.

Now, in the case of man, the potentiality of his nature as a whole is for living, not for living simply, but for the activities of a specifically human life. A human life is a whole of many activities, not only multiple in number, but various in type according to the powers and potencies from which they spring. This complex whole does not and cannot exist at any moment, for its component parts, being temporarily disposed, cannot all *coexist. The* good *of* man, which is the perfection of his nature as a whole (i.e., the complex object of all his natural desires as unified), cannot be accomplished, in the temporal domain, by any single change, or, for that matter, by any series of acts short of the work of a whole life. This is not true of any type of partial good, whether it be *a* good of man or *a* good for man, the primary or secondary object of some particular natural desire. In the light of this basic difference between the natural desire of the whole nature for its complete perfection in time, and the diverse natural desires which are identified with its distinct powers and potencies, we can see the difference between happiness, as the whole of human goods, and the various goods which constitute that whole. The plurality of partial goods arises from the plurality of objects that answer to the various desires which belong to human nature. The unity of happiness, as the complete good, arises from the unity of that complex object which answers to the desire of human nature as a whole for its complete perfection. Since the end of all desire is that which leaves nothing to be desired, happiness, conceived as the termination of man's potentiality for living humanly, is the end; and since each partial good, which can be achieved in something less than a complete life, leaves much else to be desired, it must be regarded merely as a part of happiness and a constitutive means thereto.

2. THE KINDS OF GOODS AS MEANS AND ENDS

After the student had begun to see the relation between happiness, as a whole of goods, and the various partial goods which constitute it, he might have inquired concerning the relation of these partial goods to one another. He might have asked whether all the partial goods are *equally* good, or good in the *same* way; whether one type of partial good may be a means to another, and if so, whether this means-end relationship is the same as the means-end relationship between the partial goods and happiness. These questions would have started another line of analysis. Let me briefly summarize what is involved in answering them.

A distinction we have already recognized explains why all the partial goods are not equally good or good in the same way. We have seen that the objects of desire divide into the goods *of* man and the goods *for* man, according as they are changes in man which perfect his own nature or changes in other things which are causally related to changes in himself. Now it is obvious at once that these two sorts of objects are not desired in the same way: one is desired for the sake of the other. Primarily, we desire our own perfection, and these primary objects consist of the acts and habits by which our powers are actualized. Secondarily, we desire other things in so far as these are operable by us and, as operable, capable of contributing to our own perfection. These secondary objects consist of all the physical, i.e., changeable, things which man can operate upon in one way or another, and through such operation convert into his own being. We do not desire the perfections things already possess, for *that which is* cannot be an object of *desire*, though it may be an object of *love*. We desire rather the changes which things can undergo, not for their own sake (i.e., as further perfecting these things), but for our sake, i.e., in so far as these changes are causally involved in the motions by which we are ourselves perfected. If one object is desired for the sake of another, the first must be regarded as a means, the second as an end. Hence we see that, although all the partial goods are, severally and collectively, means to happiness as the last end, one sort of partial good is also a means to another sort as an end. I shall return presently to the significance of this fact for the account of means and ends. Here I wish to consider its significance for the difference in quality between two sorts of partial goods.

That which is good as an end (even if it be not the last end or the whole good) has greater goodness than that which is good *merely* as a means. Though both may be objects of desire, one is a good to be *enjoyed* and the other is a good to be *used*. Enjoyment is the fruition of desire in the possession of the good which, prior to fruition, was being sought. An enjoyable good is, therefore, an object of desire which can be possessed. The only perfections we can possess are the perfections of our own nature — our own acts and habits. We can never possess other things except by making them part of ourselves.[25] Even so, what we enjoy is the greater actuality in us, to which they have contributed, and not a perfection relative to their natures. Changes in other things are objects we desire only to use in whatever manner is appropriate to their causal efficacy. A useful good is, therefore, an object of desire which contributes somehow to our possession of an intrinsic good, but cannot itself ever be possessed, because it is a change extrinsic to our own nature. We may speak of enjoyable goods as intrinsic because they are always changes in ourselves.

This distinction between extrinsic and intrinsic goods — or, what is its equivalent, between useful and enjoyable goods — not only increases our understanding of the difference between goods *for* and goods *of* man, but also throws light upon the traditional distinction between *bonum utile* and *bonum honestum*. This distinction is misunderstood if it is employed exclusively to divide happiness from the various partial goods; for, although happiness, being the total perfection of man's potentiality for human living, is a *bonum honestum*, it is not the only

---

25. This metaphysical meaning of "possession" must be sharply distinguished from the economic or legal meaning, in terms of which we have "property rights" with respect to other things.

bonum honestum. On the contrary, it might even be said that happiness transcends the distinction between *bonum utile* and *bonum honestum*, because whereas happiness is certainly not *used,* neither is it, strictly speaking, *enjoyed* or *possessed.* I say "strictly speaking" to indicate that the meaning of "enjoyment" or "possession" is not univocal when we speak, on the one hand, of possessing good habits or good acts, and, on the other, of possessing happiness. A good habit or a good act is something actually present and existent; but happiness can exist only as a human life itself exists — as a becoming, as a temporal disposition of successive parts. It can never be wholly present any more than a whole life can be. The distinction between *bonum utile* and *bonum honestum* should, therefore, be primarily applied to partial goods, all of which are capable of present existence. Just as happiness should not be spoken of as *a* good, which would imply that it is one among a diversity of goods rather than all of them in a certain order (for which reason we should call happiness *the* good); so happiness should be called *bonum honestum* only by an analogical extension of this signification from its primary and proper application to those partial goods which can be fully possessed and enjoyed.[26]

Restricting our attention, for the moment, to the variety of partial goods, we must now try to classify the types of good as extrinsic or intrinsic, as useful or enjoyable. Aristotle, it will be remembered, said that all goods could be divided into three sorts: external goods, goods of the body, and goods of the soul;[27] and St. Thomas approved the analysis of St. Ambrose, which divided goodness into the virtuous, the useful, and the pleasant.[28] Our first problem is to relate our twofold division to each of these trichotomies, for that will help us, secondly, to assign each type of good to its proper category.

The Aristotelian division presents only one difficulty. External

---

26. This point profoundly illuminates the distinction between temporal and eternal happiness, for the latter is *the* good which is *bonum honestum eminenter.* By comparison with eternal happiness, all partial goods can be called *bonum honestum* only analogically; and temporal happiness itself can be called "happiness" only by analogy with that happiness which can be fully possessed and enjoyed.

27. *Ethics,* I, 8, 1098b 12-15.

28. *Summa Theologica,* I, Q. 5, A. 6.

goods are clearly cases of *bonum utile,* i.e., they are all those changes in operable, physical things which, being extrinsic to our own nature, can only contribute to, but cannot constitute, its perfection. Goods of the soul (i.e., the acts and habits of those powers with which we are endowed through having a human soul) are clearly cases of *bonum honestum* — intrinsic or enjoyable goods. But what are the goods of the body, such things as health and sensual pleasure? In one sense, they are obviously intrinsic to our being: they can be enjoyed and possessed. But, even so, they are not of the same order as good acts and good habits, because they are not specifically human. They are goods intrinsic to our animal nature (the generic nature we share with brutes).[29] There is a further complication in the fact that health (though not sensual pleasure) appears to be useful, as well as enjoyable. As useful, health is *extrinsic* to the goods of the soul (habits and acts); it is a condition of human operation, and so contributes to man's specific perfection by way of material causality. Although it is intrinsic in the sense indicated, we are justified in classifying health as a useful good, along with external goods,, rather than as a *bonum honestum,* because from the point of view of those other intrinsic goods which are specifically human (the goods of the soul) health does not perfect man *qua* man, but merely helps him to achieve his characteristic perfections.

To understand the peculiar status of sensual pleasure, we must turn to the Thomistic classification. With respect to two of St. Thomas' three terms, there is no difficulty. What he calls the useful good includes everything we have classified as *bonum utile* (i.e., external goods and health, all the objects which are goods *for* man, but not goods *of* man *qua* man). What he calls the virtuous good is identical with what we have called *bonum honestum* in the restricted sense of goods of the soul (i.e., virtuous habits and virtuous acts). But sensual pleasure as a good is neither *utile* nor *honestum,* in either of these precise senses, even though it is clearly an intrinsic and not an extrinsic good, and

29. Strictly speaking, they are not goods of the "body" in the sense in which this might be opposed to goods of a living thing, goods it can possess because it has a soul and is alive. The distinction between "goods of the body" and "goods of the soul" must be understood, rather, in terms of the distinction between man's specifically human powers and those powers which man has because the rational soul virtually includes the sensitive and vegetative souls.

even though it can be possessed and enjoyed. The Thomistic discussion does not help us resolve this difficulty because St. Thomas fails to distinguish between pleasure as an object of desire (i.e., sensual pleasure) and pleasure as identical with the satisfaction of any desire. "That which terminates the movement of the appetite in the form of rest in the thing desired is called the pleasant."[30] The pleasant in this sense is not a category of good in the classification of goods as objects of desire; rather it is identical with any enjoyable good that is actually possessed. But sensual pleasure is not only enjoyable; it is desirable: it is an object of desire. To achieve a proper classification of sensual pleasure, we must, therefore, distinguish between sensible and intelligible goods. The pleasant, in the sensible order, occupies a position analogous to that of the virtuous, in the intelligible order. It is a good which can be desired for its own sake, and not merely as a means to some other partial good.[31]

Neither of the traditional threefold classifications is adequate, because three separable sets of criteria are involved: the distinction between extrinsic and intrinsic, the distinction between the useful and the enjoyable, and the distinction between the human and animal. An adequate classification of goods (which are objects of desire) must make the following divisions: (a) the extrinsic and useful, i.e., external goods; (b) the intrinsically animal and useful, i.e., health; (c) the intrinsically animal and enjoyable, i.e., sensual pleasure; (d) the intrinsically human and enjoyable, i.e., virtuous acts and habits. Of these, only the last type of good is, strictly speaking,[32] the *bonum honestum*

---

30. *Loc. cit.*, fn. 28 *supra*.

31. This is not inconsistent with the truth that sensual pleasure, like every other partial good, is a constitutive means of happiness.

32. The foregoing analysis requires us to make one further discrimination of aspects of the good in relation to appetite. Appetite may be in a state of motion toward an unattained object, in which case we speak of the good as an object of desire, and this is the good in its primary aspect. Appetite may be in a state of rest through possession of the object desired, in which case we speak of the good as the satisfactory, as the object of enjoyment, or the fruition of desire. But appetite may also be in a state of simple ordination toward an apprehended good, in which case we speak of the good as an object of love. Unlike the object of desire, the object of love is an existent perfection—the good which is convertible with the being a thing already has. Speaking theologically, God in Himself is an object of love, not of desire; the Beatific Vision is an object of desire and of enjoyment. Moreover, God, whose perfect being is perfect

hominis. The useful may, furthermore, be distinguished according as it is a means to sensible or intelligible goods — pleasure or virtue.

In the light of this fourfold classification, we can now review an

---

goodness, is the primary object of love: whatever else is loved is loved secondarily and by relation—ourselves and our neighbors as ourselves. Since what is enjoyed is a perfection possessed, the objects of love and of enjoyment may be the same (though different in aspect) in the case of loving ourselves, or others *as ourselves;* or they may may be the objective and subjective aspects of the same, as in the case of God and the vision of God. And as *uti* is divided against *frui,* so are those objects which can only be used, distinguished from those which can be loved.

It might be supposed that we would achieve clarity if we defined the object of love, not as the good, but as the beautiful. Love is that mode of apeptitive determination which abstracts from both the presence and absence of its object, and is thus distinguished from desire (for the absent object) and enjoyment (of the present object). If the good is the object of desire and enjoyment, then the good cannot be, in a strictly univocal sense, the object of love: for, since motion and rest are exhaustive, desire and enjoyment exhaust the modes of appetite with respect to the good, when appetite is simply regarded; love must, therefore, be a mode of appetite relative to apprehension, or a mode of cooperation of apprehension and appetite (of intellect and will in *amor intellectualis*). Now the beautiful is not the object of either intellect or will separately, but of both in ordered conjunction, for it is that which pleases (is enjoyed) upon being *seen* (known), as, in contrast, the good is that which is enjoyed on being *possessed.* Hence, the object of love is the good relatively, not simply, which means it is the substantial perfection of anything as apprehended, or, in other words, it is the beautiful. As its object is not the good simply, neither is love a mode of appetite simply, but rather of appetite (enjoyment) relative to apprehension of a purely theoretic sort. This explains the theological truth that it is better to love God than to know him, and better to know things than to love them, because the goodness of love is from its object, whereas the goodness of knowledge is in our mode of knowing. As the object of love, God is not the transcendant good, but the transcendant beautiful (the splendor and effulgence of perfect being); so in loving ourselves and our friends we enjoy what we apprehend as beauty of character (a work of prudence), just as enjoy the beauty of a work of art beheld. Love of the beautiful in human beings and human life explains much that desire for the good (primarily our own perfection) cannot account for: it is needed to solve the problem of altruism vs. selfishness (vd. fn. 24 *supra*), as charity is needed to supplement justice in social action.

But the object of love, unlike the beautiful, is not an object of completely disinterested enjoyment, apart from desire and action. Therefore, the object of love must be defined as the good of another person; as such it may also be an object of desire, comparable to the desire for one's own perfection. The truth that everything naturally desires its own perfection must be understood in such a way that the desire for the perfection of an *alter ego,* i. e., a loved object, is included. Just as we can never possess other things without making them parts of ourselves, so the perfection of a loved object is a perfection we vicariously enjoy as if it were the perfection of our own personality. Cf. *The Theory of Democracy,* Part II, Section 2, in The Thomist, III, 4. Although the object of love is strictly the good and not the beautiful, there remains a sense in which the loved object is, apart from desire and as simply apprehended, beautiful. To understand the object of love, either as good or as beautiful, it is necessary to distinguish the "love" which names a passion and the "love" which names a motion of the will; for in the sphere of sensitive appetite love is strictly selfish, being the origin of desire for possession, for incorporation of another into one's own being, whereas in the sphere of will, love is entirely altruistic, being correlative with desire for the good of another as other and reaching fruition in the apprehension of that other's perfection as beautiful.

earlier enumeration of partial goods.[33] There were, we said, five kinds of good: wealth, bodily goods, social goods, habits, and activities. We used the word "wealth" to signify all external things which are useful goods *for* man. "Bodily goods" signified such objects as health and sensual pleasure, the status of whose goodness is also clear. But what are the things called "social goods" — friends, a peaceful community, etc.? Clearly they are human, not animal, goods, but it is not so clear whether they are useful or enjoyable, extrinsic or intrinsic. It seems possible to view social goods in both ways. As I shall try to show subsequently, the social goods are, in their primary aspect, instances of the *bonum honestum hominis,* though, in a secondary aspect, they may also be regarded as extrinsic and useful, i.e., *as means to virtue.*[34] With respect to the two remaining goods (habits and activities), there is no problem of classification: they are intrinsically human and enjoyable. There is, however, a problem about what makes a habit or an act good rather than bad. The student might have raised this problem by asking why *every* habit and act is not good, since by definition the good is the actualization of a potency, and every habit and operation is such an actualization. What, then, is it which makes some acts and habits good (virtuous) and others bad (vicious)?

Although this is an extremely difficult problem (perhaps, the most difficult question about the relation between the metaphysical and moral significations of "good"), I shall briefly suggest a solution in terms of two points already made. In the first place, the real, as opposed to the apparent, good is always the natural good as apprehended. Now, although any habit or act may be apprehended as an apparent good, only certain habits and acts can be truly apprehended as goods, because they alone conform to the natural good of our powers. As themselves determinate natures, as well as being determinate properties flowing from our essential nature, the several powers do not tend toward any

---

33. Vd. Chapter III, *supra,* pp. 40-42.

34. Vd. Chapter VII, *infra.* One indication that social goods should be classified primarily as intrinsic and enjoyable goods is that friends are objects of love—having a goodness to be loved as we love the goodness of ourselves. Cf. fn. 32 *supra.* Another indication is that the goodness of a community, domestic or political, is a common good in the sense that it is shared by the members: it is not only a common object of desire, but also a fruition commonly enjoyed. Vd. *The Theory of Democracy, loc. cit.*

actualization as good, but only that actualization which corresponds to each power's nature. This is most simply seen in the case of the intellect as a power of knowing the truth about things. Because it is by nature a power of *knowing,* acts and habits of *knowledge* are its natural good, whereas acts and habits of error are naturally evil, and hence can be apparent, but never real, goods. This accounts for the distinction, in the sphere of intellectual habits and acts, between the virtuous and the vicious. There is another group of habits and acts, which are called "moral" as opposed to "intellectual" (not moral as opposed to *immoral*), because they are not habits and acts of knowing or thinking, but habits and acts of desire or social conduct. Here the criterion for the distinction between good and bad lies in the fact that our powers of conscious desire or behavior are moved by the apprehension of some object as good. But our intellectual judgments concerning the good may be true or false, and, accordingly, the good apprehended may be real or apparent. Hence only those acts or habits of desire (whether on the part of the will or of the sensitive appetite) are virtuous, which are determined by the apprehension of the real good. The same must be said for the virtuous in the sphere of social behavior. The traditional maxim that the virtuous, in the case of moral acts and habits, is that which is in conformity with reason must be interpreted to mean, not the power of reason simply, but the power of reason as perfected by good habits, by knowledge rather than error. When it is remembered that the truth of practical judgments (about good and bad) is by conformity with right desire, there will appear to be circularity, but this is avoided by the fact that conscious desire is itself right by conformity with natural desire. In short, the natural good is the ultimate criterion whereby the virtuous and vicious are distinguished.

In the second place, human powers are principles of many acts and capable of multiple habituations. Furthermore, the unity of man as a substance implies, as we have seen, the unity of his powers as ordered to one another, and hence the unity of their actualization through co-operation and co-habituation. These facts explain why vicious habits are bad, even though each by itself is the actualization of a power. For vicious habits conflict with one another, as well as oppose the formation of virtuous habits, whereas virtuous habits are, *inter se,* thoroughly harmonious and mutually supporting. Hence vicious habits *prevent* the maximum actualization of human powers, whereas virtuous habits tend toward such maximization. Thus we see (in the case of habits, though not with respect to acts) how the moral criterion of virtue and vice relates to the metaphysical criterion of goodness as actuality of being.[34a] The perfection of man as a whole requires the maximum actualization of his powers. Granting that habits are actualizations, the "metaphysical goodness" of any habit taken by itself is specious because neither powers nor their habits exist separately; hence only morally good habits are metaphysically good as making for the perfection of man as a whole.

I have now outlined the sort of answer which must be given to the student's question about the kinds of good, and their inequality due to differences in type. But he also asked about means and ends — whether one partial good is a means to another of different type in the same way that all partial goods are means to happiness. This question must now be briefly answered.

At one point in our earlier discussion, we distinguished between two sorts of means: constitutive means (parts of a whole) and functional means (one partial good as means to another).[35] The difference between these two sorts of means is readily grasped by comparing, first, their respective ends and, second, the relation of the means thereto. In the case of constitutive means, the end is always happiness, or the whole good, and here the means is included in the end it serves, serving it by effecting its partial realization. In the case of functional means, the end is always another partial good, and here the means lies outside the end it serves (as the efficient cause lies outside the effect), for it serves its end by working as a condition precedent to the realization of the end. So much is clear; but the student may wonder whether all functional means are useful goods, and whether their ends are always one or another sort of *bonum honestum*. Unfortunately, the truth is not that simple. One type of good may function as means to another good of the same type, as well as be a means to goods different in type. Thus, wealth may be a means to health, or health to wealth, and both to

---

34a. Cf. St. Thomas's discussion of the meaning of "*good*" in the case of *good habits: Summa Theologica*, I-II, 55, 4 ad 2.

35. Vd. Chapter IV, p. 48, *supra*. The second sort were not then called "functional means."

pleasure; and, within the large group of goods we have classified as wealth, instruments of production may be means to consumable goods; furthermore, virtuous acts may be means to good habits, virtuous habits means to good acts, and both may be means to social goods, as well as be served by them. In the order of partial goods, there is a great complexity in the functional relationships of diverse types of goods as means to ends. This complexity can, however, be reduced somewhat by the following observations: first, that some partial goods are never functional means, but always ends, notably, sensual pleasure and certain good acts which are good quite apart from the formation of habits of conduct; second, that the same good may function as a means in relation to some other good as an end, and be an end served by some other good as a means, as health, for example, in relation to virtue and to wealth; third, that even when functioning as means certain goods are essentially ends, such as virtuous acts and habits, whereas certain goods are essentially means even when functioning as ends, such as wealth and health; finally, that only those partial goods which are essentially ends are essentially constitutive of happiness, whereas those which are essentially means are accidentally constitutive of happiness.[36]

Within the domain of partial goods, it is also important to disin-

---

36. These last two points are of great importance, for they apply to the analysis of functional means the deeper principles whereby goods are distinguished as *utile* and *honestum*, and as human and animal. In one sense, of course, every functional means is useful, but a good may be useful functionally (in relation to some other good it serves) without being essentially useful in its own type(i.e., not being a good *for* man, but a good *of* man). Furthermore, since happiness is specifically human, only those goods are essentially constitutive of it, which, as partial goods, are *bonum honestum hominis;* extrinsic goods, or intrinsically animal goods, are only accidentally constitutive of happiness.

These two points convey Aristotle's insights about means and ends. He distinguished between goods which are mere means, goods which are both means and ends, and the good which is absolutely and simply the *end*. A mere means is any *bonum utile*, whether or not it also *functions* as an end; a means which is essentially an end is any *bonum honestum;* with the exception of pleasure in the sensible order, and contemplative activity in the order of intelligible goods, happiness is the only good which never functions as a means, and it is the only end simply and absolutely, because even pleasure and contemplation are constitutive means of human happiness. Aristotle also distinguished between antecedent and constitutive means, and this is the distinction we have made among partial goods (all of them constitutive in a broad sense) according as they are accidentally or essentially constitutive of happiness. In other words, a mere means is, as constitutive, accidental to human happiness, whereas a means which is also genuinely an end is essential to the constitution of human happiness. These two basic points go much deeper than the distinction among partial goods as functional means and ends. Vd. Aristotle, *Ethics*, I, 7. Cf. John Dewey's attempt to regard *every* good *equally* as an end, in *Reconstruction in Philosophy*, New York, 1919: Ch. VII.

guish between the universal and the particular, i.e., between the type *as such* and singular instances of each type. Failing to do this, we cannot understand the constitution of happiness; for when it is said that happiness includes *all* good things, what is meant is goods of every type, and not every possible instance of each type of good. This must not be construed, however, to mean that happiness is actually constituted by types of good, rather than by singular goods actually possessed, for we know that universals do not *really* exist in the moral order, any more than in the physical order, except through singular embodiments. Happiness may be conceived (i.e., exist in the ideal or conceptual order) in terms of the order and variety of types of good (i.e., universals); but happiness cannot occur (i.e., exist in the real order of living itself) except through the actual possession of goods, and these must all be singular instances of the several types. We are compelled, therefore, to define a a third kind of means. As the various types of good are the constitutive means-in-general of happiness, so singular instances of each type are the constitutive means whereby that type of good is gradually realized in the course of life. These means-in-particular (*this* commodity, this pleasure, *this degree* of virtuous habit, *this* good act, etc.) are thus each directly constitutive of a special type of good, and through serving as means in this way, they are indirectly constitutive of actual happiness. Whereas the constitutive means-in-general are necessary means of happiness, the constitutive means-in-particular are contingent means, for no one of them is indispensable to the realization of its type, or of happiness as a whole, as, on the contrary, every type of good is indispensable to the realization of happiness.[37]

There is, finally, a fourth type of means — the most important of

37. All the objects of choice are means of this type. We always choose and act in particular situations, and the good which is the object of choice is always, therefore, a singular instance of a type of good—hence always a constitutive means-in-particular. (This classification of all objects of choice as constitutive means-in-particular does not prevent the cross-classification of them as functional means or ends.) This fact about the objects of choice is indispensable to an understanding of freedom of choice. Only means-in-particular are contingently constitutive of happiness; means-in-general, being necessarily constitutive, cannot be objects of *free* choice. In willing happiness necessarily, we must will whatever is necessary to its constitution, as we conceive it; but we need not will this or that particular instance of a type of good, for such means are only contingently constitutive of happiness. Failure explicitly to observe this distinction between constitutive means-in-general and -in-particular accounts for some ambiguity in passages in which St. Thomas discusses the necessitation of the will with respect to means. Vd.

all, because it both epitomizes what is involved in the notion of means (i.e., something practically useful) and combines the highest degree of utility with the greatest excellence a means can have as an intrinsic good. I shall call this fourth type of means the generative or productive means, the end in this case being happiness itself. As one partial good may be functionally related to another as means to end, by the productive relation of efficient causality, so there is one sort of partial good —and only one — which is functionally related to happiness itself by direct efficient causality. I am referring here to the cardinal virtues — the moral virtues and prudence. This type of good (virtue simply or absolutely, in contrast to intellectual virtue, except prudence, which is virtue only relatively or secondarily) is at once a *bonum honestum* and also the most useful sort of productive means, precisely because what it serves functionally as an end is not another partial good, but happiness itself. Before considering the relation of virtue to happiness, let me summarize the four sorts of means-ends relationships, according to the principles which determine them: [38]

---

38. Four things should be noted about this classification of means: first, that the same good may be both a constitutive means and a functional means, for the cardinal virtues are both constitutive of and generative of happiness; second, that as a constitutive means a good may be enjoyable, though as a functional means the same good is useful—thus, virtues and good acts are both useful and enjoyable; third, that the same good may be a functional means, both generally considered and specially considered, for the cardinal virtues are both productive of good acts, and of happiness itself; fourth, whatever good is a functional means, whether productive of another partial good or of happiness, must be a means-in-particular, for functional relationships occur only in the existential order.

It should also be noted that the means-end relationship is causal, and that constitutive means belong to the order of material causality, their ends being formal causes—wholes or universals, which can be concretized or embodied; whereas functional means belong to the order of efficient causality, their ends being final causes. Hence functional means partake more of what is essential to the notion of means, than do constitutive means; and cardinal virtue more so than any other partial good.

Finally, and above all, it should be noted that anything which is a means to virtue is *indirectly* productive of happiness (the state or political common good being, as we shall later see, chief among such indirect productive means); and the basic distinction in the aspects under which the same partial good is regarded as both constitutive and productive, whether of happiness itself or of some other partial good, is a distinction between that good as enjoyable and as useful (thus, virtue is both constitutive and productive, both an enjoyable and a useful good, both an end and a means).

Summa Theologica, I-II, 10, 1; 10, 2, ad 3; 13, 6, ad 1; cf. *Ibid.*, I, 82, 2. It should be added that, although all means-in-particular are contingent goods, so far as the constitution of happiness is concerned, not all are mere means, for some are ends, being instances of types of good which are essentially constitutive of happiness, because intrinsic human goods (i.e., *bonum honestum hominis*, such as *this* good act, or *this* *degree* of a virtuous habit).

I. *Constitutive means:* realizing the whole of which they are parts.

    A. Constitutive means-in-general: realizing happiness as a whole.

    B. Constitutive means-in-particular: realizing a universal type of good directly, and happiness indirectly.

II. *Functional means:* productive or generative of the end they serve.

    A. Functional means, generally considered: any partial good which is productive of another partial good as *an* end, whether same or different in type.

    B. Functional means, specially considered: cardinal virtue, the only partial good which is directly productive or generative of happiness itself as *the* end.

3. VIRTUE AS PRINCIPAL MEANS TO HAPPINESS

When the student understood happiness as *the* end in relation to which all other goods are means in one way or another, he would also understand that happiness is the first principle of moral theory. But he might still be unable to see how the first principle theoretically determines the subsidiary principles of ethics; and, more that that, he might remain quite perplexed about how the theory worked in practice. Knowing *what* happiness was, he might still wonder *how* to become happy.

The theoretical question is the easier to answer. If the first principle of any practical science is the end, the secondary principles are the means. Just as the conclusion is implicitly contained in the premises, so knowledge of the means is contained in knowledge of the end. We cannot know what happiness is without knowing its constitutive means: according as men differ in their conceptions of the order and variety of goods, so will they differ in their definitions of happiness; and the truly adequate definition of happiness will be adequate in its enumeration of the partial goods and true in its ordering of them. But the constitutive means, taken as a whole, are identical with happiness: only by a purely formal definition of happiness, can it be conceived apart from the goods which constitute it.[39] Hence the constitutive means are not the secondary principles of moral theory. The secondary principles must be functional means. Just as for any partial good as *an* end, there must be generative means, so for the whole good which is *the* end, there must be means specifically able to produce happiness. Furthermore, from knowing *what* happiness is, we should be able to determine the nature of the means productive of it. When we make this determination, we shall have solved the only remaining problem of ethical theory, and this will enable us to consider its significance for practise, i.e., *how men become happy.*[40]

The deductive determination of the secondary principles of moral theory can be simply accomplished. Happiness is an *order* of goods. Throughout the course of life, the various partial goods which constitute happiness cannot be adequately obtained unless they are sought in the right order — an order which proportions them according to their worth as goods and respects their functional relationships. But no good whatsoever can be obtained except through activity. And activity with respect to goods as objects of desire is determined by acts of the desiderative faculties, either the will or the sensitive appetite. Hence we see that happiness will be obtained only if activity flows from right desire. This becomes a self-evident truth when we understand "happiness" as a *right order of desirables* and "right desire" as a *right ordering of desires.* But good habit is the proximate principle of the good operation of any power. Good habituation of the appetitive faculties is, therefore, the source of good acts of desiring and these determine good activity with respect to objects of desire. We must conclude that good appetitive habits are the principal means to happiness — the means directly pro-

---

39. A definite "order and variety of goods" is *materially* what happiness as "all good things" is *formally.* Cf. Chapter IV, pp. 55-56, *supra.*

40. The two theoretical problems of ethics concern, first, the end; and second, its generative means. The first problem is solved when happiness is adequately and truly defined; the solution is here equivalent to knowledge about the order and variety of partial goods, and their functional relationships to one another. The second problem is solved when we are able to *deduce* from the nature of happiness what *must* be the nature of its generative means. Knowledge of the constitutive means is explicitly equivalent to knowledge of the end; but knowledge of the generative means is only implicitly contained in knowledge of happiness, and must be deductively explicated. When we know *what* the generative means are, we can proceed to the practical problem of *how* to possess *them* and, through them, how to become happy.

ductive of it. As earlier analysis showed, the moral virtues are good habits of desire and of behavior in accordance with right desire. When each moral virtue is understood as a habit of rightly ordering one's desires in relation to happiness as a right order of goods or desirables, it will be seen at once that no one of the moral virtues can be possessed except in the same degree that all are possessed. Moreover, since habits of right desire are formed and become operative with respect to particular goods, they depend upon the making of a right choice among the particular goods which are contingent constitutive means. Prudence as a virtue of practical reason is a habit of rightly making such choices. Hence, just as one moral virtue cannot exist without all the others (or can exist only in the same degree), so no moral virtue can exist without prudence, or it without them: right desire for the end (i.e., desire for the right end) is indispensable to a right choice of particular means, since these are good only as realizing the kinds of goods which are the constitutive means-in-general of happiness; and right choice of the particular means is indispensable to the formation and operation of habits of right desire for the end. If now we use the word "virtue" to signify the cardinal virtues (the several moral virtues and prudence) in their integrity, we can formulate our conclusion by saying that virtue is the principal means to happiness — or, more strictly, the only means adequate to the task of directly generating the end.[41]

In the order of theory and intention, the end precedes the means,

---

41. By the "integrity" of the cardinal virtues is meant their functional interconnection, their co-existence in the same degree of effectiveness as generators of the end. The proof that such integrity is necessary can be made either from the unity of the end which these virtues serve as productive means, or from the fact that each of the moral virtues depends upon prudence, and it depends upon all of them. It is, therefore, true to say that if a man habitually does any sort of act for the completely right reason, he is a man of perfect virtue, for he will do every other sort of act in the same way. Cf. Aristotle, *Ethics*, VI, 13. Proceeding from happiness as the end and first principle, we arrive at the conception of virtue as the productive means and second principle. In this deduction, only the virtue of prudence is specified; the notion of moral virtue as a good habituation of the appetites, as their rectification by a right ordering of all desires, precedes the specification of moral virtue by the definition of the distinct virtues of temperance, fortitude, and justice. If this deductive procedure is followed, the integrity of virtue will be understood before the specific moral virtues are distinguished. Aristotle's failure to proceed in this way permits readers of his *Ethics* to misunderstand the essence of virtue; for only after the integrity or unity of virtue is understood, can anyone distinguish between apparent virtue (i.e., one "virtue" existing apart from others) and real virtue.

In his Preamble to *Summa Theologica*, II-II, St. Thomas says: "We may reduce the whole of moral matters to the consideration of the virtues."

for it is by knowledge of the end that we know and can intend the means productive of it. But, in the order of practise and execution, the means precede the end, for in order to become happy we must first acquire the productive means. Whereas the constitutive means *are* the end so far as it is realized at any time, the productive means *are* the end in process of becoming realized. Because the end determines the productive means (in the order of intention) and the productive means determine the end (in the order of execution), it is equally true to say that as man conceives the end, so will his character be; and to say that as a man's character is, so is the end for him.[42] As reciprocally determinative of each other, the end and the productive means are corelative: the order of goods or desirables is correlative with the ordering of desires. If the end at which a man aims is only the apparent, and not the real good (because of some inadequacy or falsity in his conception of the variety or order of partial goods), then his habits of desire may *appear* to be virtuous, but they will really be vices; and conversely, if a man be habitually vicious in *any* respect, that disorder of his desires will be productive of *apparent,* but not real, happiness. The man of really good character is not one who possesses some virtues and some vices, for no *real* virtue can be conjoined with any vice. Only the cardinal virtues in their integrity can constitute a really good character, just as only an adequate and true ordering of all partial goods can constitute real happiness. Thus we see the two ways in which happiness *exists practically.* Theoretically, happiness may exist in the mind as a conception of the end, whether true or false. But practically, it exists either (a) *objectively* in a human life in so far as it is perfected by the possession of all good things, or (b) *subjectively* in a human character in so far as it is perfected by real virtue. This is just another way of saying that the productive means are the end in the process of becoming. But saying it this way enables us to see that though the complete actuality of happiness is attained only in a complete life, it is virtually present, as *in its causes,* in a good character. Objectively, happiness exists only as a process of becoming exists, which means that it cannot exist at any moment; whereas subjectively, happiness exists at any moment to what-

---

42. Cf Chapter IV, p. 68, *supra.*

ever extent its efficient causes exist. In the first sense, therefore, we can-not say that a man was happy until he is dead; in the second, we can say that he is happy while he is alive, if we know that he has a virtuous character.

Human nature, through its powers, is the principle of operation, of all the activities of human living. A man's character is his second nature, especially in view of the integrity of virtue as a cohabituation of his powers. As human nature is the principle of any sort of opera-tion, good or bad, and hence of good or bad living, so a good charac-ter, as a man's second nature, is the principle of good operations, or happiness as a life well lived. In proportion as his nature is perfected by virtue, so will a man's life be perfected by happiness.[43]

Only two problems remain, one theoretical, the other practical. The theoretical problem concerns the intellectual virtues — habits of knowl-edge and skill. Clearly, they are among the partial goods essentially constitutive of happiness; clearly, they are, in functional relationship to other partial goods, both means and ends — both generative of good intellectual activity and generated by it, as well as, indirectly, by other means, such as health, social goods, and moral virtue. But just as clearly, we know, from what they are and from what *the* end is, that the intellectual virtues (always omitting prudence) are not productive means with respect to happiness, except indirectly, perhaps, in so far as

---

43. This reasoned truth of moral philosophy must be submitted to the criticism of the theologian who considers all moral problems in the light of the dogmatic truth about man's fallen nature. Cf. fn. 1a *supra*, in which moral philosophy, as a work of reason, was discussed in relation to moral theology, as based on revelation. Moral philosophy proceeds on the hypothesis of the natural man. If this hypothesis be false, as revealed religion declares, then all the conclusions of moral philosophy must either be regarded as hypothetical, or they must be qualified and transformed by subalternation to theo-logical truth. The fundamental problem here is whether purely natural virtues are ade-quate for the achievement of the natural end, the good which is proportionate to the nature; and this turns on whether, in the case of fallen human nature, the cardinal virtues can be *really* possessed at all (i.e., in their integrity) without the help of grace and infused moral virtues. If not, then temporal happiness is unattainable except for natures elevated by grace; but, on the other hand, if grace makes possible the integral possession of the natural virtues, then it not only enables a man to direct his life toward a supernatural end, but also enables him to possess natural virtue in such a way that the temporal happiness, due his nature, can be achieved. With God's help a man can live well on earth if, but for the grace of God, he cannot.

they are involved in the formation of moral virtue. That is why, in the classification of good habits, the moral virtues and prudence are called cardinal, or virtues simply, whereas the speculative virtues and art are called secondary, or virtues relatively. It is not merely that the intellectual virtues confer only an aptitude for good work, but not an habitual performance of good acts. The deeper reason is that the intellectual virtues perfect a man's nature only in certain respects, making him a good scientist or a good artist, and able to operate well in these domains of work; whereas the cardinal virtues perfect a man's nature with respect, not to some limited good, but all good things or happiness, making him good as a man, and also making him live his whole life well. If the essence of any virtue as a partial good lies in its being a generative means, then those habits which are productive of happiness are virtues simply; in contrast, those habits which are productive of only another partial good (i.e., intellectual activity) are virtues only relatively.[44]

This fundamental insight about the intellectual virtues helps us to resolve an apparent conflict between two traditional definitions of temporal happiness. The apparent inconsistency originates in Aristotle's *Ethics*. In Book I, Aristotle defines happiness as activity in accordance with perfect virtue, in a complete life, accompanied by a minimum sufficiency of the goods of fortune. In Book X, happiness is defined as one sort of activity, contemplative activity or the activity of the speculative virtues. If the second of these definitions be taken as saying what *constitutes* happiness, then it is clearly contrary to the first definition, and clearly false; for the intellectual virtues are certainly not "perfect virtue" or virtue simply, and if happiness *consisted in nothing but* contemplation or speculative activity (all other goods being merely auxiliary or antecedent thereto), then such happiness would falsify the *formal* definition of the end — that which, when possessed, leaves nothing to be desired. The first definition of happiness is, on the other hand, veri-

---

44. If, however, the essential goodness of a virtue be the actualization it confers upon a power, then the intellectual are superior to the moral virtues because they perfect the highest power of man. Cf. St. Thomas, *Summa Theologica*, I-II, 66, 3; 66, 5, ad 1; 66, 1.

fied by this same criterion: if, in a complete life, attended by good fortune, a man acts in accordance with perfect virtue (i.e., the integrity of
the cardinal virtues), his life will become happy through the possession
of all good things. Now, "all good things" includes intellectual virtues,
and contemplation, or good speculative activity, in accordance there-
with. The man of perfect virtue so orders his desires, and so acts, with
respect to the order of partial goods, as to possess intellectual virtue in
some degree, and put these virtues to use in good activity. Hence the
second "definition of happiness" can be reconciled with the first on the
condition, of course, that it be subordinated thereto. This is done by
seeing that it is not, strictly, a definition of happiness at all, but rather
a statement of what is the highest good in the order of partial goods.[45]
Because the intellect is man's highest power, the operations which flow
from its good habituation are the highest form of human activity. In the
order of partial goods, then, contemplation or speculative activity is
highest; intellectual virtue is better than moral virtue because directly
generative of such activity; and all the other partial goods, both extrinsic and intrinsic, must be ordered to the achievement of intellectual virtues and to their exercise. Even the moral virtues and prudence, regarded as generative means *within* the order of partial goods, must be
regarded as aiding the attainment of wisdom and the activity of contemplation.[46] But the moral virtues and prudence do not discharge
their total generative function *within* the order of partial goods. As
productive of happiness, they also stand *outside* the order of goods —
functioning uniquely as the efficient cause whereby all good things become possessed in a life well lived. When we speak of happiness as a
life of virtue we must, therefore, mean two things; first, that it is a life
generated by activity in accordance with cardinal virtue; second, that it

---

45. It should be remembered here that happiness must never be called "the highest
good" if that phrase be taken as signifying the highest type of partial good. Being the
whole of goods, happiness cannot be highest in the order of goods which constitute it,
though in this order of goods itself, one good can be higher than another, or highest
of all. Vd. Chapter IV, p. 55, *supra*.

46. Vd. St. Thomas, *Summa Contra Gentiles*, III, 37; cf. *Summa Theologica*, I-II,
66, 5 ad 1.

is a life which *includes* the highest form of activity in accordance with intellectual virtue.[47]

The other problem which remains concerns the acquirement of virtue in its integrity. The cardinal virtues which generate happiness must themselves be generated by good acts. How this can be accomplished is the central *practical* problem in ethics. It is solved only by rules which are inexact and relative to different types of individuals living under different circumstances. The theoretical level of moral philosophy goes no further than definition and analysis of ethical principles — happiness and virtue. But moral theory, even if it be perfectly formulated, is inadequate to direct a man in the acquirement of virtue and the attainment of happiness. A man may know, *theoretically,* all about happiness and virtue, and nevertheless fall far short of being virtuous and happy, because he does not know how to apply this knowledge in his own life. Moral theory is practical only in the sense that it underlies the formulation of rules which are genuinely practical as directive of conduct. On

---

47, Thus the apparent conflict between Book I and Book X of Aristotle's *Ethics* is resolved. If it was due to any fault on Aristotle's part, it can be attributed to his failure to distinguish between two senses of "the highest good"—(a) the sum of goods, which is happiness as *the* end, constituted by every type of partial good, and generated only by cardinal virtue; and (b) the supreme type of partial good, which is contemplation, as the end served by all the other partial goods, though generated directly only by intellectual virtue. There can be no question that it is the goodness of a whole life, not speculative activity, which is the ultimate object of natural desire, and hence is happiness or *the last end.* Speculative activity is merely the best aspect of a good life, its most enjoyable phase. This is confirmed by Boethius' definition of happiness as the state of those who possess in aggregate all good things. Thus conceived, happiness cannot be identified with any single type of good, not even with speculative activity *in this life.* I say "in this life" because Boethius's definition reveals the analogy of temporal and eternal happiness (the one constituted by a simultaneous, the other by a successive, possession of "all good things"), and thereby helps us to understand how the contemplation of God in the Beatific Vision may be identified with eternal happiness, whereas no sort of speculative activity can be rightly identified with temporal happiness. In this life, the contemplation of God, whether it be the activity of wisdom as a purely natural virtue or the activity of faith and supernatural intellectual gifts, is not happiness, but only the highest part thereof. Hence two things must be said about St. Thomas' definition of imperfect, or temporal, happiness as consisting in contemplative activity: first, that this is not an accurate definition of temporal happiness, any more than Aristotle's definition in Book X is; second, that it is a better definition of the highest part of temporal happiness, than could have been given by Aristotle, because St. Thomas conceives contemplation in terms of God as the object, and as supernaturally generated by faith and the gift of wisdom, whereas Aristotle's meaning for "contemplation" lacks any objective specification, and even if the Divine be implied as object, merely natural wisdom is obviously insufficient. Cf. *Summa Theologica,* I-II qq. 3-5.

the one hand, without theoretically true principles, practically wise rules could not be formulated; for unless the nature of virtue and happiness is understood, how can particular acts be well regulated toward their achievement? On the other hand, without practical rules, the truest principles are inadequate in the practical order, and even sound rules require the work of prudence for their application. But these practical rules are not capable of universal or exact formulation; and prudential judgments are seldom articulated even by the man who makes them.[48]

The man of virtue has practical knowledge of the means and end of life. Through his moral virtues he has a connatural knowledge of the good at which these virtues aim; and through his prudence, he has a living habit of regulating each particular act in accordance with the demands of virtue. But if having virtue is indispensable for knowing practically how to live well — if virtue itself mediate between true theory and sound practise — then how can virtue be acquired? Since theoretical knowledge of principles is insufficient, since practical knowledge of some sort seems to be both *prerequisite* for the formation of virtue and also *consequent* thereupon, there appears to be a vicious circle here, or at least a mystery about how anyone becomes virtuous. So far as I know, there is only one solution to this problem, in the domain of purely natural causality. One man of virtue, thereby having practical knowledge, not only for the guidance of his own life, but for the direction of others, must be the efficient cause of the formation of virtue in another man, so that the latter gradually becomes able, through the practical knowledge which virtue gives, to regulate his own life. It remains true, of course, that the principal efficient cause of virtue must be a man's own acts, performed voluntarily and directed with prudence by his own reason. The moral preceptor is, therefore, like any other teacher, at best an accessory or cooperative cause: moral training, like intellectual teach-

48. Aristotle's remarks about the inexactitude and relativity of practical knowledge must be regarded as applying only to the rules of conduct, and not to our knowledge of the principles, which knowledge is theoretic in mode, though practical in end and object. It is only knowledge which is practical in mode, as well as in end and object, that is intrinsically inexact and relative to the individual practitioner. Vd. *Ethics*, I, 3; II, 2. Cf. our prior discussion of the relativity of practical judgments (Chapter II, pp. 27, ff. *supra*), their status as opinion, and the significance of this in correcting the error of Socratism and Hedonism, which supposes that theoretic knowledge of the good commands good acts unfailingly.

ing, is an art of cooperating with nature, aiding the primary cause which is reason's own activity. So far as habituation is concerned, the efficiency of moral training can go no further than the formation of what Aristotle called "inchoate virtue" — moral habits formed in one person as the result of the regulation of his acts by another. The growing person may thus come to possess inchoate virtue before he knows the principles of moral theory and before he has practical knowledge whereby to regulate his own conduct. Such inchoate virtues, nevertheless, operate as the seed of genuine virtue, for they are a source of good conduct; and as the result of good acts, though these be initially performed under external regulation, connatural knowledge of the good accrues, practical knowledge of how to act well grows, and prudence itself develops.[48a] By this route, it is possible for a man to become virtuous without ever being learned in moral theory. No one ever *becomes* virtuous simply by learning moral theory, though moral theory may confirm a man in virtue, or remotely facilitate his practise of good acts.

In the light of the foregoing, we understand why Aristotle made ethics a branch of politics — at least to the extent of viewing the legis-

---

48a. What is called "inchoate virtue" is not, properly speaking, virtue at all; yet it is a condition antecedent to the achievement of virtue. To understand the stages on the way to becoming virtuous, we must first distinguish the antecedent dispositions, which are improperly called "virtues," from the genuine habits which may be consequently formed, and which are properly virtues. We must further distinguish, among the antecedent dispositions, those which are natural and those which are acquired: the natural dispositions toward virtue are those temperamental inclinations to good acts which Aristotle called the "temperamental virtues" (vd. *Ethics*, VI, 13); in contrast, there are acquired inclinations toward good acts, resulting from extrinsic training in the domestic or the political community: these are the "inchoate virtues"—not properly virtues because not, strictly speaking, habits formed by the exercise of prudence on the part of the agent. Finally, we must distinguish, among those habits which are genuinely virtues, the imperfect from the perfect. Unlike dispositions, some of which may be natural, all habits are acquired; the distinction here, between imperfect and perfect virtue, turns on the disconnection vs. the connection of the several cardinal virtues. No single virtue is *perfectly* possessed, unless *all* are possessed *in some degree*. Not only is the acquisition of any single virtue gradual, but so is the achievement of the integrity of virtue itself. In the temporal order, natural dispositions precede and condition the formation of "inchoate virtues" or acquired tendencies toward good acts; these in turn precede and condition the formation of genuine habits, whether these be virtues imperfectly or perfectly. The inchoate virtues provide an inclination to the right end, enabling prudence to begin to operate in the choice of means, and thus initiating the formation of genuine virtues. Without such dispositions formed by extrinsic training, there could be no beginning of real virtue. (For St. Thomas s discussion of natural inclinations toward virtue, vd. *Summa Theologica*, I-II, 58, 4 ad 3.) Cf. fn. 41, *supra*, and fn. 53 *infra*.

lator as a moral preceptor, and the just laws of a good society as causes of virtue and happiness. The government of others, whether domestic or political, can be best accomplished by those who know the principles of ethics, and who also, through being themselves virtuous, have practical knowledge whereby to formulate sound rules. The theoretical study of ethics is, therefore, primarily for the government of others, and only secondarily for the enlightment and guidance of those who have already begun the life of virtue.[49] If moral principles are primarily put into practice by the statesman, we should be able to find in them the foundations of political philosophy.

---

49. Herein lies the significance of Aristotle's statement that it is difficult, if not impossible, to teach ethics (even the theory) to the young, in whom virtue is not formed, and who have insufficient practical experience of "the facts of life." Vd. *Ethics*, I, 3. Cf. *ibid.*, II, 1, 1103b 1-5; X, 9. Cf. St. Thomas's discussion of the role of law in training youth: *Summa Theologica*, I-II, 95, 1.

CHAPTER VII.

FROM ETHICS TO POLITICS: THE COMMON GOOD
AND DEMOCRACY

ON THE PRACTICAL LEVEL, ethics is auxiliary to politics in so far as the knowledge it affords is *useful* to the legislator or magistrate. When Aristotle speaks of politics as being the architectonic discipline in the practical order, his criterion is the *use* of knowledge to direct action. But, as we know, there is a theoretical level of practical knowledge, concerned with universal principles, with the definition and analysis of end and means. On this level, ethics is architectonic and politics subordinate. Political *theory* is a part of moral philosophy. Though politics has some principles peculiarly its own, their truth can be verified only by reference to the prior principles of ethics. Just as the principles of physics (i.e., the philosophy of nature) are not *first* principles, but subalternate to metaphysics, so the common good, which is the first principle of political theory, cannot be understood except in the light of virtue and happiness. In other words, the political common good is *an* end, but not *the* end: it is an end, in a certain order, but also a means to happiness, which is the end *absolutely*.[50] Thus, our inquiry in the field of morals, having established happiness and virtue as the first and second principles of ethics, leads us to the foundations of political philosophy, for it enables us to see the common good both as an end and as a means. All of political philosophy rests upon this insight because, unless the common good is the end of political activity, there is no answer to *realpolitik;* and unless the common good is itself only a means to happiness, there is no answer to "totalitarianism" — using that word

---

50. I say "political common good" because in one meaning of the phrase "common good" happiness is a common good—a good common to all men because they are specifically the same in nature. The political common good is also a good which is common in that sense, but, in addition, when the phrase "common good" is used in the restricted political sense, it means the goodness of the political community as such. In what follows, I shall use the phrase "common good" only in this restricted sense to mean "the welfare or well-being of the community itself."

for the false political doctrine that the State is the highest good or the whole good in the temporal order.[51]

To establish the foundations of political philosophy (by refuting *realpolitik* and totalitarianism), it is necessary to understand the nature of the state, and the precise character of the goodness which inheres in the political community. The first of these problems concerns the origin of the state and its mode of being. The second requires us to define the common good by locating it under one or another of the categories in terms of which we have already classified the types of partial good. By doing this, we shall be answering a question, previously raised, about the precise character of the social goods.

(1) *The nature of the state.* If man were not by nature a social, and also, through being rational, a political, animal, the state or political community would not itself be natural. It originates, or comes into being, in answer to a human need. If man, like other non-gregarious animals, could subsist in a solitary mode of life, not even the family would be a natural community, for it would answer to no natural need. And if man could live well (i.e., live humanly, rather than merely subsist), apart from a larger community than the family, the domestic society would suffice, and there would be no natural need for the state. That which comes into being as indispensable to the fulfillment of a natural need is itself natural and necessary. This type of naturalness

---

51. I undertook the dialectic of morals as an effort to overcome moral skepticism and hedonism on the part of contemporary students. Vd. Chapter I, pp. 7-10, *supra*. As I pointed out, skepticism about the objectivity of moral truths necessarily leads to the adoption of *realpolitik*, which is skepticism about the objectivity or universality of political principles. Vd. fn. 9 *supra*. Furthermore, just as the student who is a skeptic about moral matters is also usually a hedonist in his explanation of moral phenomena (i.e., the facts of preference), so those who adopt the position of *realpolitik* are usually advocates of totalitarianism—even if they would be shocked to discover this. Even those who think they oppose totalitarianism, because they magnify the "rights of the individual," affirm its basic tenets when they claim that all "moral values" are relative to the *mores* of the community, for then there are no independent moral criteria by which the community itself can be criticized as good or bad. Furthermore, just as hedonism is the error of converting a partial good into the whole good (treating pleasure as if it were happiness), so totalitarianism is the error of similarly converting a partial good—treating the State as if it were *the absolute end*. In the dialectic of morals, I did not attempt to criticize every variety of error in ethical theory, but only to answer the moral skeptic and the hedonist; so here, in considering the foundations of moral philosophy, I shall try to refute only *realpolitik* and totalitarianism. Other fallacies in political doctrine can be readily corrected by anyone who knows the right principles.

and necessity is in the order of final causality. To say that the state is natural in this sense is, therefore, to deny that it is artificial — i.e., an accidental contrivance which is totally dispensable, as, for example, any work of useful art that is a mere luxury. At one extreme, then, there is the error of the social contract which conceives the state as if it were a mere luxury — not natural at all in the order of final causality. At the other extreme, there is the erroneous notion that the state is entirely natural in the order of efficient causality — that it flows from instinctive determinations, rather than is a free work of reason. This latter error confuses human association with the instinctively determined communities of the social brutes. The nature of the state is rightly conceived only when it is understood both as originating in natural needs, and also as being a mode of association which is determined by reason rather than instinct.

The needs which the state satisfies can be briefly enumerated by reference to the partial goods which constitute happiness. Man cannot live well without a minimum sufficiency of external goods (wealth) and without health (an intrinsic, though animal, good) : though these can be provided by the domestic economy, the ampler economic facilities of the political society, through greater division of labor, can guarantee them more readily. (Hence Aristotle says that though the family and the village can supply the wants of daily life, the state is better able to meet these same needs, by extending and regularizing the economic functions: the state satisfies these needs on more than a day-by-day basis.[52]) Wealth and health do not suffice. Man cannot live well unless he lives virtuously — unless he has good habits and operates accordingly. But the life of virtue is itself a social life because man is by nature a social animal: this applies not only to the moral virtues, as principles of social behaviour, but also to the intellectual virtues, which are formed and operate through the communication of men with one another. Man is both rational in his social proclivities, and social in the exercise of his rationality. Now the structure of the domestic or tribal community cannot provide an adequate social setting for the acquirement or exercise of virtue, moral and intellectual. Because it is a

---

52. Vd. *Politics*, I, 2.

more complex and diversified organization, only the political community can adequately provide the conditions of virtuous living, through the peaceful unity of a multitude of men, greatly diversified in the quality of their endowments. (Hence Aristotle says that the state, which originates in the bare needs of daily life, continues in existence to provide the conditions of a good, or virtuous, life.[53]) We see, therefore, that the social goods, among which the goodness of the political community is paramount, function as means to all the other partial goods which constitute happiness.

Everything which is natural exists in some way. To complete our understanding of the nature of the state, we must ask about its mode of being. That which exists primarily is a substance, and when we speak of natures, in the primary sense, we mean the essential natures of existing

53. Vd. *Politics*, I, 2, 1252b 27-30. One point should be stressed, namely, that the acquirement of the moral virtues depends, as we have seen, upon good government. Cf. Chapter VI, p. 106, *supra*. Wise regulations, in the domestic community, and just laws, in the political community, are indispensable as extrinsic, efficient causes for the production of the virtues in an inchoate form; and inchoate virtue is, in turn, a necessary stage through which the individual must pass in becoming genuinely a man of virtue. Furthermore, because man is not simply rational, because he is an animal, a creature of passions, reason needs external help in enforcing its own rule upon the appetites. The good which reason may truly apprehend exercises authority over his actions, but this authority is unsupported by enforceable sanctions. This is the essential defect of ethical eudamonism, for, considering the individual in isolation, the pursuit of happiness cannot be enforced: a man cannot impose extrinsic sanctions upon himself; he is not forcefully *obligated* to become happy; he is not duty-bound by risk of punishment. This defect is, of course, remedied by considering the individual in relation to his fellow men, with whom he is associated in the political community. Since other men, as well as himself, depend upon the common good for the pursuit of happiness, he is obligated to act for the common good; and his social duties, enforced by political sanctions, operate reflexively to support the rule of reason in his own private life. Purely moral authority being authority divorced from power, the good as apprehended exercises only moral authority over a man's actions; authority combined with power being effective sovereignty, the state exercises sovereignty over human life. Sovereignty—and the obligations, duties, and sanctions which it institutes—is indispensable in the moral order because man is not purely a creature of reason. There are, in short, two sorts of *natural* authority: The moral authority of a man's own reason, which imposes only *intrinsic* obligations upon his will and his acts, and the political authority of a sovereign (i. e., a man's community), which obligates him *extrinsically*, and enforces duties by sanctions.

Even political sovereignty, the theologian tells us, is not sufficient, when we consider man's fallen nature. Though virtue is the intrinsic principle of good acts, two extrinsic principles are required for the formation of virtue: direction (i.e., law) and help (i.e., grace). In making this point, St. Thomas means by law, not merely human law, but Divine law, proceeding from the sovereignty which God exercises over human life. Cf. fn. 47 *supra*.

substances. The state is certainly not a nature in this primary sense: it is neither a substance nor the essential nature of one. Now, whatever else exists, other than substances and their essential natures, must have some accidental mode of being. Hence, the state exists accidentally. This is confirmed by its very nature as an organized multitude, for this reveals it to be a form of composition or order — an accidental form through which a substantial many is unified. Though it belongs properly in the sphere of prudence rather than of art, the state has the same kind of accidental being that a work of art has (e.g., a house is an accidental unity, realized through a form of composition and order). But every accident must exist in some substance: it cannot exist by and of itself. Thus, works of useful art exist as accidental determinations of natural inorganic substances. Since it is an enduring association of men, a state must exist as an accidental determination of the natures of its members. Not being natural in the order of efficient causality, the state cannot exist in human powers as such. The fact that it is a work of reason indicates that it exisits in the habits of men — by rational determination of their powers. In so far as the state is itself a good, it must exist in the good habits of its members; and since the habits in question must be habits of social behavior, we reach the conclusion that a state exists (a) accidentally, (b) in the sphere of habit, (c) through the moral virtues as principles of just conduct, without which (d) the peaceful association of a multitude acting for a common good is impossible. Justice is not merely one of the moral virtues, along with fortitude and temperance; justice, generally considered, is all the moral virtues as integrated and in their social aspect, i.e., as principles of social behavior. Hence, the state exists through and in the justice of its members, differing from virtue itself (which also has an accidental mode of being) in that virtue exists as the accidental determination of a single human nature, whereas the state exists as the habitual co-determination of the natures of a multitude of men.[54]

---

54. As an unjust law is a law in name only, being really an expression of force, so a state not founded in the justice of its members is a state in name only, being really an organization of violence, in which some men dominate others by force and the others submit through fear. Though an association of men through force and fear may endure for some time, it lacks the unity of peace which prevails only when all the members work for a common good. When men are organized by violence, those who

(2) *The goodness of the common good.* The preceding analysis of the nature and mode of being of the state enables us now briefly to define its characteristic goodness. In the first place, since its very naturalness and necessity is in the order of final causality, we know at once that the state *is* itself a good, i.e., an object of natural desire, responding to the needs of man's rational, social nature. In the second place, since its mode of being is in and through the virtues of the multitude, we know that the state *is identical* with the common good. Just as virtue is an individual good (i.e., a good existing in a single individual), so the state is a common good (i.e., a good co-existing in a multitude of individuals). It is, therefore, false to say that the end of the state is the common good, unless the "common good," here mentioned, signifies happiness. The common good, which is identical with the well-being of the state (i.e., with that unity of peace which distinguishes the goodness of the state from the evil of violent organizations), is the end of government, i.e., of political activity both on the part of rulers and of ruled. In the third place, just as the virtues are partial goods constitutive of happiness, so is the common good a partial good: it is the greatest of the social goods. Moreover, since it is analogous to virtue in its mode of being, it has an analogous mode of goodness; it is an intrinsically human good and a *bonum honestum.* (This is true of all the other social goods.) In the fourth place, although in the order of partial goods it is inferior to intellectual virtues and contemplative activity, serving these goods as do the moral virtues, the state is indirectly productive of happiness, through being directly productive of moral virtue, i.e., forming inchoate virtue, applying sanctions to reinforce virtue, pro-

---

wield force exercise it for their private interests, and the rest are enslaved. (Of course, even the just society requires government with enforceable sanctions: those who do not act justly out of conscience must be compelled by fear of the law. Cf. fn. 53, *supra.*)

The definition of justice throws light on this point. As temperance is the habit of foregoing immediate pleasures for the sake of a greater good, as fortitude is the habit of suffering immediate pains for the sake of a greater good, so justice, as a special virtue, is the habit of not willing an excess of good for one's self at the expense of a diminished good for others. And justice, generally, consists of all the virtues directed simultaneously to the good of others and to one's own good through being directed to the common good in the fruits of which all equally share. "Justice," said Aristotle, "is the bond of men in states, for the administration of justice is the principle of order in political society" (*Politics,* I, 2, 1253a 37).

viding the conditions for virtue's exercise. Whereas any partial good may function as a generative means with respect to some other partial good, the state, like moral virtue, stands in a peculiar relation to happiness, the whole of goods. Finally, from all this we know that the political common good, in the sense defined, is not identical with happiness: the goodness of the state as such is not the supreme good in the temporal order, for it is neither the highest good in the order of partial goods, nor is it equivalent to "all good things" — that which, being possessed, leaves nothing to be desired. On the contrary, the essential goodness of the state, like the essential goodness of moral virtue, lies in its productive function with respect to happiness.[55]

Although the goodness of the state, or common good, is not *the* end in the temporal order, it may, nevertheless, be *an* end, in the strict sense in which every partial good which is a *bonum honestum* is an end. Moreover, within the sphere of specifically political activity, the common good, the welfare of the political community, is *the last end* toward which all political institutions, agencies, and acts, are ordered as means. In the domain of political life, the common good occupies a place analogous to that of contemplation in the order of partial goods constitutive of happiness. Furthermore, the common good is a complex whole of many social goods, whose variety and order constitute it, as happiness is constituted by the variety and order of all good things. And just as moral virtue is both a constitutive part of happiness and also its productive means, so good government is, as a social good, constitutive of the common good, and also the one means which is directly productive of the state's well-being. (By "government" here I understand all the institutions and agencies through which both rulers and ruled can act for the common good.) Just governmental activity not only maintains the common good, but also facilitates the formation of virtue

---

55. Though the state appears to be a whole, of which its human members are parts, the goodness of this whole is not greater than the goodness of the parts, i.e., the perfection of their being by happiness. On the contrary, the goodness of this whole (i.e., the common good) is, along with other social goods, a constitutive part of happiness, even though happiness appear to be the good of a part (i.e., the perfection of a single human life). Though the common good be the good of a whole, i. e., the community, it is not the whole of goods, for that is happiness. There is nothing paradoxical about this

in the citizens and thus the state is, *indirectly,* productive of happiness, or the life of virtue.

This indicates at once the major principles of political theory: the first principle is the end (the common good), the second principle, the productive means (good government), analogous to the first and second principles in ethical theory (happiness and virtue). The exposition of political theory consists, therefore, first, in a definition of the end and an analysis of its constitution; and second, in a definition and analysis of the productive means. As there are several species of virtue, so there are specifically distinct forms of government, though here there is a basic difference in that, whereas the specific virtues are conjunctive and must be integrated, the several forms of government are disjunctive and cannot co-exist. The central problem in political theory is the

---

when one remembers that the individual man is a substance, whereas the state is nothing but an accidental being. Just as the perfection of a man (happiness) is greater than the perfection of any of his powers (virtues), because the goodness of a substance in being and operation is greater than the goodness of an accidental being and a principle of operation; so happiness is greater than the common good—including it as a partial good, and subordinating it, along with virtue, as an end subordinates its productive means. (On the ambiguity of "common good," vd. *Summa Theologica,* I-II, 90, 2.)

Traditional statements to the contrary, suggesting that the good of the state is greater than the good of its members, as the good of the body is greater than the good of its parts, can be accounted for by the error of neglecting the fact that the state is not a substance, nor are its human members substantial parts of a substantial whole. Though the error is made by Aristotle (vd. *Politics,* I, 2, 1253a 19-24 and *Ethics,* I, 2, 1094b 7-10), though it is repeated by St. Thomas in places too numerous to cite, the source of the fallacy is in Plato's conception of the state by analogy with the soul, in the *Republic.* It is a profound historical misfortune that Aristotle, whose greatest achievement in metaphysics was the notion of substance, did not employ this notion to purify his own political thinking of Platonic reminiscences. This error, combined with a failure to understand the nature of temporal happiness, has led some scholastics to suppose that the State, or the common good, is the supreme temporal good, from complete subordination to which man can be saved only through his ordination to God and the supernatural good of eternal happiness. Vd. Father John McCormick, *The Individual and the State,* in Proc. Am. Cath. Phil. Assoc., XV, pp. 10-21. Cf. J. Maritain, *Freedom in the Modern World*: pp. 49-53. Only religion can save man from totalitarianism. This may be true *practically,* but it is certainly not true *theoretically,* for by principles known through reason alone, we know that temporal happiness is the end which the state must serve, and that the natural perfection of man's life, as *the* end in the temporal order, subordinates the political common good, both as a constitutive and a generative means.   This truth is not inconsistent with that other truth, namely, that under cerain circumstances and in certain respects, the individual's well-being must be sacrificed for the welfare of the community, especially when the existence of the community is threatened by external aggression, the very fact that such sacrifice can be justified only by extraordinary circumstances indicates that *normally* the good of the individual is paramount.

classification and evaluation of the forms of government, and here the crucial question is whether one form is better than another, *on moral grounds,* because it is essentially more just, through greater justice effecting a greater common good and, ultimately, making the state serve the happiness of *every* man, rather than that of the many or the few. This question will be answered in the affirmative, despite traditional opinion to the contrary, once it is seen that the common good is the end of government, not of the state, and that happiness, which is the end of the state, is, as a life of virtue, necessarily a political life. When the forms of government are specified by criteria of justice (the distinct elements of political justice being separable and cumulatively combinable), they can be graded according to their moral goodness and democracy can be demonstrated to be, on moral grounds, the best form of government[56]—intrinsically, the most just; extrinsically, productive of the most complete common good and, thereby, of human happiness.

Thus we have learned that the nature of the state, its mode of being, and its essential goodness, cannot be understood except in terms of the nature of man, the perfection of his nature by virtue, and the perfection of his life by happiness. Unless, therefore, the principles of ethics can be ascertained, as objective theoretical truths comprising wisdom in the practical order, the principles of politics cannot be established. Unless, as a branch of practical philosophy, it be founded upon moral wisdom, political theory cannot be defended against the skepticism of *realpolitik,* or protected against the doctrinal errors of totalitarianism. But no part of practical philosophy (ethics or politics) can be validated as knowledge of absolute and universal principles without the prior acknowledgment of ultimate theoretic truths — about being, goodness, and the nature of man. To overcome moral skepticism, and *realpolitik* as its consequence, it is necessary, first, to eradicate its root in the prevailing positivism which denies philosophical knowledge —

---

56. Vd. my paper, *The Demonstration of Democracy,* in Proc. Am. Cath. Phil. Assoc., XV, pp. 122-165; my answer to Dr. O'Neil, *The Demonstrability of Democracy,* in The New Scholasticism, XV, 2, pp. 162-168; and a series of articles, by Father Walter Farrell, O.P., and myself, under the title, *The Theory of Democracy,* beginning in The Thomist, III, 3. Many of the points here barely indicated, concerning the nature of the *common good* and the character of temporal happiness, will be therein expounded with greater analytical detail than was possible in this brief statement.

metaphysics, and especially the philosophy of man. This has been illustrated in the very motion of our inquiry; the dialectic of morals uncovered the need for a prior dialectic of substance, essence, and man. Until that prior work is done, most of the truths we seemed to reach, both dialectically and by deductive elaboration, will not convince the student. Lacking conviction with respect to these, the student remains susceptible to all the "political religions" which rush in to fill the vacuum created by his doubts and denials. In the world as it is today, a good work the philosopher can do is to labor inductively in the fields of metaphysics and psychology, for the sake of moral wisdom and, ultimately, for the foundation of a true political philosophy.